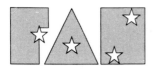

Collected and introduced by
RITA CARTER

Drawings by John Ireland

COLLINS
8 Grafton Street, London, W1
1983

William Collins Sons and Co. Ltd
London · Glasgow · Sydney · Auckland
Toronto · Johannesburg

Fanmail
1. English letters
I. Carter, Rita
826'.912'08   PR1347

ISBN 0 00 216528 7

First published 1983

Set in Sabon and Univers Light by
Rowland Phototypesetting Ltd
Bury St Edmunds, Suffolk

Made and printed in Great Britain by
St Edmundsbury Press, Bury St Edmunds, Suffolk

Contents

List of Contributors

Abba 129, 142.
Larry Adler 68, 69.
Peter Alliss 77.
Jeffrey Archer 130.
April Ashley 36, 86.

Robin Bailey 47, 152.
Peter Barkworth 32.
Tracie Bennett 26.
Jeffrey Bernard 110, 111, 112, 114.
Sir John Betjeman 119.
Acker Bilk 44, 45.
Cilla Black 18.
Reginald Bosanquet 82.
Raymond Briggs 61, 159.
Sue Brown 94, 132, 133.
Dr Rob Buckman 78.

Peter Bull 144, 145.

Rita Carter 22, 41, 56, 70, 71, 113.
Barbara Cartland 33.
Peter Christie 33.
Jilly Cooper 62, 63, 135, 148.
Tom Crowe 49.

Paul Daniels 141.
Hunter Davies 102, 120.
Len Deighton 104.
William Donaldson 66, 67, 108, 160.
Dorothy Dunnett 122, 123.

Sandor Eles 42.
David and Elizabeth Emanuel 100, 101, 136, 137.
Douglas Fairbanks Jnr. 30, 31.

5

Introduction

However bad a performer, somewhere there's someone who has taste that's even worse. It's nature's way of making sure that everybody who exercises their talent in public has at least one person – The Fan – to keep them going. In order to fulfil their function, sooner or later fans must Get in Touch. And get in touch, bless 'em, they do.

I should say that I speak as a fan myself, qualified by years of unrequited love for various famous men. My first fan letter was sent to Richard Greene, the dimpled and waven-haired television Robin Hood of the mid-1950s. 'Dear Richard Greene,' I wrote, 'I think you are very handsome.' Unable to think of anything else to say I ended, predictably: 'Please may I have a picture of you?' and received by return a black and white postcard-sized photograph of Greene, dimpling like mad around an upended longbow. I duly pinned it on my bedroom wall and kissed it goodnight each evening. But this, my first contact with an Adored One, left me obscurely dissatisfied. I had a feeling even then that the process of expressing adoration held greater potential than this unremarkable little exchange suggested.

The ritual grew a little richer when my fickle five-year-old favours transferred from Richard Greene to another Channel 9 swash-buckler, Robert Shaw, alias Dan Tempest, pirate captain in *The Buccaneers*.

Shaw was my first True and Lasting Love, an early blueprint for Mr Right and one that set an impossibly high standard. Love blossomed each Wednesday at 5.15 pm and took about twenty seconds to reach full, heart-stopping, bloom. First there was the establishing long-shot – a pirate galleon riding proud on a storm-tossed ocean. Then the slow zoom-in to Captain Tempest standing on the deck, his strong features profiled against the setting sun. Then the clincher: Tempest swung to face camera . . . a zoom-in to close-up on the sea-tempered face . . . the steel-blue eyes . . . the secret smile playing at the corners of his lips ... Oh, Captain Tempest – what storms did you precipitate in my infant breast!

'Dear Mr Shore,' I wrote earnestly after a particularly stirring Wednesday drama. 'I know I cannot marry you because you are so old. By the time I am old enough to marry you you will probably be dead. Never mind. Please can I have a coloured picture of you? With your name written on it. By you.'

I can't remember what, if any, reply I received to this charmless little note. I do recall, though, that soon afterwards *The Buccaneers* was taken off the air and a great void opened in my life which was briefly and unsatisfactorily visited by Sir Launcelot (Channel 9 again); Robert Horton; (a very early) Clint Eastwood and – so fleetingly he hardly counted – Cliff Richard. On these faint idols I practised my fan-letter-writing until, by the time another Great Love hove into view some years later, I was an expert at this particular type of gentle harassment.

This time the victim was a somewhat limited actor who had been chosen by a budget-conscious casting director to play the lead role in a television thriller which enjoyed a moderate success in the early 1960s. The part called for an Angry Young Man, and this actor demonstrated how angry he was by a curious sniffing action – just one nostril at a time – meant, I suppose, as a sniff of contempt. Unfortunately it had the effect of making him look like a rather worried rabbit. At that time my fantasy life was divided pretty equally between imagining myself the Adored One's Chosen One (pre-emancipation, this involved being rescued a lot) and being the Adored One himself. In the latter flights I went around sniffing with furious contempt, particularly at my mother, who ended up taking me to see an ear, nose and throat specialist.

Meanwhile the object of this adolescent idolisation was subjected to all the disadvantages of mass-admiration without any of the usual advantages (as soon as the thriller finished he resumed one of the longest rests in acting history). After I had written him so many letters ('Do you wear pyjamas in bed?' ... 'Do you like blondes or brunettes?' ... 'What do you eat for breakfast?') that he wisely stopped replying, I bribed or cajoled packs of twelve-year-old girls to write to him for me. For the price of a Mars bar, a couple of correct geometry answers or the *actual* words of the dirty bit in Lady Chatterley, I'd be given the replies, study the signature minutely, note with excitement any deviation from the standard lines ('How kind of you to write. I am very flattered by your comments, and enclose, herewith, a signed photograph of myself'), and add the photo to the vast number that already covered my bedroom walls.

Due to me, the man was forced to have made up not one, but *three* sets of portrait photographs. As a seasoned fan I knew my rights, and one of them was to get a different coloured photograph at least once every six months. At one point he wrote:

> Dear Rita,
> You now have fourteen signed photographs of me (Type One) and five (Type Two). I am shortly to place an order for a further set of prints. Perhaps you would give me some idea of your future requirements so I can order accordingly.

(I replied that I thought ten would be enough.)

I also discovered his telephone number (it was in the London directory – going ex-directory had not, until then, been a precaution warranted by the state of his career). I plagued him with emotional, sometimes tearful, phone calls, until he first arranged to have his calls intercepted by a stern operator, and later changed his number. The campaign culminated with me leading a solemn pilgrimage of schoolgirls to the south London mansion block where he lived. We sat balefully on the garden wall eating strawberry-split ice lollies, failed between us to find a brave enough spirit to knock on his door, and went home Uplifted for having looked upon his Dwelling.

My love for this actor was extinguished only for lack of fuel. The *Woman's Own* Information Service provided me with a complete list of his credits – some eight films, mainly supporting features, which I diligently tracked down one by one to suburban fleapits throughout the home counties.

I watched spellbound as my hero guffawed, threw a chicken leg over his shoulder and grasped a passing wench in a medieval melodrama; marvelled at his physical prowess as he leapt from a getaway car in a cops'n robbers; was fairly sure I spotted him demonstrating an elegant seat astride a piebald pony in a spaghetti western (the feathers made it difficult to be certain); and noted (with only a passing thought to the ENT specialist) that he continued to sniff contemptuously, even when playing a non-angry police con-stable in an Ealing comedy. I sat through each film three, four . . . up to half a dozen times. But it wasn't enough. The members of the fan club deserted . . . the BBC refused to repeat the thriller in which he'd starred, and my contemporaries, even those who had spurned the charms of Presley and Richard, now swooned at the Beatles. In the mid-1960s a whole new era of hero-worship began, when fans were counted in millions and fan letters by the ton, and a whole new industry grew up to feed off the excess passions of teenybopper fanatics.

That industry still ticks along, though it's not as crazily exploitative as in the days when IPC launched a new magazine every month, each one wholly dedicated to the breakfast preferences, vital statistics and other essential information about a single sixteen-year-old, fresh-out-of-the-mould pop star. Pop stars *are* still mass-marketed, but most of today's fans relate to the performers as equals, not as idols. The groups, like ABBA, which *do* still receive traditional fan mail, quite literally by the ton, do not actually receive very *interesting* letters. And so you'll find very few letters to pop stars or groups in this book.

In fact there are very few 'fan' letters at all. My original idea was for a collection of letters of admiration. I once came across one – still the classiest fan letter I've ever discovered – which was sent by Charles Dickens to the publishers of his contemporary, George Eliot (Mary Ann Evans). Dickens had just read Eliot's *Scenes of Clerical Life*. He wrote:

> . . . the exquisite truth and delicacy, both of the humour and of the pathos of those stories, I have never seen the like of, and they have influenced me in a manner that I should find very hard to describe to you if I had the impertinence to try.
>
> In addressing these few words of thankfulness . . . I am, I presume, bound to adopt the name that it pleases that great writer to assume. I can suggest no better one; but I should have been disposed if I had been left to my own devices, to address the said writer as a woman. I have observed what seem to be such womanly touches in these moving fictions, that the assurance on the title page is insufficient to satisfy me even now. If they originated with no woman I believe that no man ever before had the art of making himself, mentally, so like a woman, since the world began.

I hoped that an appeal to contemporary artists might uncover similar modern examples of witty, perceptive or elegant fan mail, albeit from less illustrious hands.

Accordingly I wrote to every well-known name I could think of. The initial list of addresses was rather arbitrary. My friends were confronted with the demand: 'Name twenty famous people,' and my colleague Rosemary Atkins and I included all the people we personally admired, regardless of whether they were likely to get interesting fan mail. The list thus tended at first to reflect our own areas of interest – pretty light on sportspeople, for instance, but heavy on certain kinds of authors and sexy politicians. Later drafts were more comprehensive; eventually we reckoned to have approached practically every famous living British person.

My letter to them asked if they had received (or written) any letters of admiration which they considered striking. I added that I was also interested in *any* type of letter if it was amusing, moving, bizarre, or even outrageously rude. I added the last category for good measure, but I ended up getting more of that type than any other, with the result that the book evolved into a celebration of the outrageous, the dotty and the eccentric. In asking for letters of admiration I had failed to reckon with two factors: one was the modesty of talented people, and the second was the predictable content of most expressions of admiration. Straightforward fan letters make pretty tedious reading for all but the two people most closely involved.

Thus, people were, on the whole, far quicker to offer for publication damningly critical letters than flattering ones. Modesty was probably the main reason, but I think too that people feel the more they publicise cruel criticism of themselves, the less potent the criticism becomes. Nasty letters *do* hurt and successful people are not immune from the pain (although long exposure to them does have a certain anaesthetising effect). Throw the hate-mail in the wastebin and it whispers away at you for years. Expose it to other people – people who recognise it for the nonsense it is – and its power is undermined.

Rude letters, on the other hand, tend to be funny. Very few people can express disapproval without exposing some deep vein of pomposity or indignation. Definitely Disgusting is Alive and Well and living, actually, in Worcester Park, from where she (or he) wrote to Jilly Cooper (page 62). Jilly, incidentally, receives a vast amount of mail – ninety-nine per cent of it from readers who are delightedly knocked out by her work. Jilly says she is keeping the letters to read as consolation in days ahead when nobody buys her books. It's just as well such days are never likely to arrive, because I suspect she would find the fan letters dull, if flattering, reading. It's the one per cent of shocked, horrified, and disapproving letters which are funny, and that's why it's these which appear in this book. The same is true of the letters sent to columnist Jean Rook – there seems to be a direct correlation between the degree of sparkle a writer puts into his or her work, and the pungency of their critics. Even Gerald Priestland generates some distinctly un-Christian responses from his listeners after some of his more forceful radio or television talks.

There can't be many projects which involve writing to practically every 'household' name in the country (though the handful of people who replied wearily that they received letters like mine the whole time may think there are *too* many). It was, in itself, a fascinating exercise and one which bore out many personal prejudices in a thoroughly satisfactory way. All the people I always thought looked nice sent nice replies, and the few I thought not so nice, didn't. It also proved many old saws: the busiest people were often the first to respond and the most willing to find time to help (Barbara Cartland replied with three neatly extracted examples of mail by return of post). The higher their repute and the greater their talent, the more gracious and kindly, invariably, was their response. With a handful of exceptions, everybody was generous with good wishes for the project – even those who couldn't, or preferred not, to contribute.

Some of the replies to my letters were themselves amusing. Actor Michael Bryant couldn't supply anything because, he said, 'Yours is about the most exciting letter I've ever had.' Tom Conti wrote characteristically, 'Exhibiting my mail is not something I feel compelled to do.' Roy Kinnear offered to send me any nasty ones he received in future in the hope that I'd deal with them for him; and James Villiers regretted that he couldn't contribute because he received only love letters. Polly Toynbee reflected that the age of *belles lettres* seemed to have passed her by ('I suppose people don't write to me because I don't write to them') and television vet Christopher Timothy had thrown his away. (He did recall one, though, from a woman who wrote a six-page castigation of him – his acting, his appearance, his voice, his private life . . . and finished, triumphantly: 'You're not even any good as a vet!')

Arthur Marshall returned my letter with a scribbled comment 'FAR TOO BUSY.' Then, obviously thinking that sounded rather harsh he added, 'I'm quite nice really!' Marghanita Laski said she didn't contribute to other people's non-creative books (and pointed out that I hadn't sent a stamp for her reply). Auberon Waugh said the same thing (though not mentioning the stamp) more elegantly. Kingsley Amis seemed to think I wanted him to *write* the book, and hoped that everyone I approached would reply in as curt and dismissive a way as he. An editorial assistant in the Guinness Superlatives office (which absorbed the letter intended personally for Norris McWhirter) sent a letter of stunning pomposity, stating that they would not pass on any of their bazaar *(sic)* letters to me in case their correspondents felt betrayed. (Surely someone aiming for the Guinness book of records is not shy of publication?) It ended by wishing me 'success, among those who have no such fiduciary inhibitions'.

Richard Ingrams put his letter from me into the Letters column of *Private Eye*, under a heading which implied I was copying *The Letters of Henry Root*. The result was a deluge of letters from would-be Roots, offering me copies of letters *they* had sent to famous people, sometimes with replies. A couple of them offered their work for publication 'in return for some of the folding stuff'. Most just wanted to get published. One man had been 'doing a Root' for twenty years – his persona a 'humble railway guard' from Ruislip. Many of his letters had found their way into the local newspaper letters page: 'To many passengers, purchasing a season ticket is like throwing a cocktail party or barbecue, to impress the neighbours and friends . . .' 'It is over two years since I had a letter in the *Gazette* suggesting that Ruislip Residents' Association had been infiltrated by extremists . . .'

I have included one letter from this writer in this book. As far as I know it's the only one of its type. I can't guarantee that, though, because among the people who allowed me to look through their correspondence files was Henry Root himself, alias William Donaldson.

The Letters of Henry Root encouraged hundreds of imitators, many of whom chose Root himself as the target of their efforts, and Donaldson's mail is full of Root pastiches, many of them very clever. Amongst them is the odd letter addressed to the person behind Root, and one or two of these appear here. If, however, I've been taken in and the writer was in fact intending a Root-like hoax on the creator of the wet-fish King, the joke's on me.

I've tried to keep out letters which are embarrassing, exploitative or sad. In compiling the book there were, anyway, two automatic guards against material like that creeping in: one, that the letters were selected and contributed in the first place by their recipients; two, that wherever it was possible to contact the writer I asked, and was given permission, to use their work. I have rejected one or two letters even after they'd passed these filters because I felt publication would be unfair to the writer. If, despite this, you come across any letter which offends your fiduciary inhibitions, I'm sorry. I hope you don't, and that you'll enjoy reading them as much as I enjoyed collecting them.

Fans are fickle friends. I once had one called Arthur. Arthur was a Chelsea pensioner with a cat called Pearl and a touch of arthritis in winter. He was 'ninety-seven years young' and professed for me Undying, Total, Dedicated and Unswerving Loyalty – often several times a day. Sometimes my pigeon-hole would be so full of letters from Arthur (lovingly labelled S.W.A.L.K. or sometimes longer and more obscure ciphers which I didn't wish to work out) that I'd be forced to write and forbid him to send any more for a week. Which only brought about a greater deluge later. Arthur wrote to me thus for nearly two years. Until, one day, he stopped. As the weeks wore on and still there were no SWALKed envelopes from Arthur, I started to fear for his welfare. I tried to recall the state of his arthritis last time he'd written . . . fretted at the thought of what might have happened to Pearl. . . . Then, one day I happened to go to another part of the newsroom where other reporters have their pigeon-holes. And noticed that my colleague Trish Ingrams had a particularly heavy postbag . . . each one labelled S.W.A.L.K.

Here are some fan letters which I think amusing. They range from hot and lusty to coolly approving. One that I think goes right Over The Top is this, from Down Under. It was sent to Cilla Black:

Love Fantasia to Cilla Black   New Zealand

Oh. Let me rape your flower-temple in your sweet exceeding
    loveliness.
Yea, that most beautiful garden, tho' so marred by men.
And thou' your face blossom in repulsive physical ugliness –
    dear, I'm ever amazed!
Your soul is like an eastern palace garden raining scarlet
    roses, rare sky-blue carnations, *yellow* 'pearls',
Oh I cascade upon your perfumed Breast, as tho' you were,
    beloved, truly you.
Your silver unicorn soul does ring with rose blossoms like an
    immortal sea,
Truth weeps and wakes upon your pearly breast, like
Gardens of the soul cascading flowers.
Music flames like a love's troubador, her pageantry of
    Emerald Gold.
My Lovely! singing 'mid the royal red red roses!
Pouring like a beautiful fey her haunting 'palace' of her
    jewelled sea –
Drip down your bosom like an apricot sky, oh poignant
    cypress of the mystical aquamarine waters,
Nightingale warbling to the emperor-white disciple,
Who seeks like a brilliant peacock in his solitary, restless
    dream,
Communion with your snowy soul, and with your Fair, an
    ever-truthful body-soul.

Soul-body or gossamer Lark a-fainting down the pearly rose-
pink green-tinged stairs of ecstasy – mingled with rare sky
blue;
Shimmering Barque of Music's sweet instantly cascading
like an emerald waterfall –
Locked in her scarlet embrace – My Beautiful Beloved For-
evermore.

From Dilys

*To Mary Whitehouse, from a young admirer at Gordonstoun
School:*

Gordonstoun School
26th May 1982

Dear Mrs Whitehouse,

I hope you are well, I am just writing to say what a jolly good
job I think you do. It takes a very strong character to go out
into the eye of the decadent thousands and say what you
think is right. My friends and I just wish there were a few
more knights like you to stop the wickedness of pornography
and all abuses of the body. Well done! Do you think I could
have a picture of you for our study wall, I am sure it would go
well beside our picture of Mrs Thatcher. I enclose a stamp for
postage.

Yours most sincerely,
J. P. Wenham

To Barbara Cartland:

Benevento, Italy
7th October 1981

Devine Barbara Cartland,

I am an Italian admirer. You are a leader by way of beauty, intelligent in every way nature intended. You are wonderful: unequalled by any woman on earth not even by those of your age or of those much younger. You are an angel from Heaven. I say again that I am a fervent admirer and I pray for your well-being and progress and I wish you happiness, immense wealth and luck in anything you do.

A rather backhanded compliment, this, to Andrew Gardner and me. Together we read the news on Thames television's nightly news programme Thames News *for nearly five years:*

Thanks to you all

Dear Andrew and Rita

Thanks for reading the news to Us most Nights
I wonder if you both know just what chukles
We have at home when we find your lines
Have got mixed up with your pictures on some nights

Watching you both politely trying not to laugh
When reading the wrong lines that has been
Mixed up well and truely by the lads
These little misshaps makes you both seem real
As reading all the sad and happy news
Must sometimes be a straine

But with a smile like yours
Neither of you can go wrong
We often wonder just what you tell
Francis when he gives up the weather
Thats often glumy and seldome hot
Watching you all have a lough
When the news is over
Chatting about the things that has
Gone wrong that Night?

These Jubilee Celebration lines (contributed by their author) were sent to the Queen by the keeper of a well-wishing computer at Cambridge University:

Celebrets

WEN queend is nottis lizabe
For norgetall inglist
Extrinken lorfor reuded we
Supposen trule nottist

Thile jubill arles custor cell
Forionay abourp
Ne wilip fiven nover twell
Ho Queen agaitle sourp

Poempe blebrat eless clas
Who tracept wilant ting
Siump not quee blodd virit as
To sand this oustor wing

Her Majesty, it seems, was Amused:

Buckingham Palace

Dear Mr Parington,

I am commanded by the Queen to thank you for your letter of 16 November – and the peom (written at one remove?) by yourself, to mark the Silver Jubilee. Her Majesty appreciates this interesting, if somewhat obscure, tribute, and sends you her thanks for it.

This, to Judith Hann, was definitely not *written by computer:*

To Judith

Hey Judith, You smashing young darling;
When I see you, I sing like a starling.
You're more tasty than wine
Made from fruit of the vine
Or Black Label Lager by Carling.

Whenever you come on the box
I go soppy right down to my socks.
You're a cinch of a rose
From the tips of your toes
Right up to your lovely dark locks.

Kevin

Another Judith Hann admirer:

Leeds
20th May 1982

Dear Ms Hann,

Tomorrow's World is certainly one of the better television programmes, always interesting and informative and sometimes amusing.

However, I must confess that part of my enjoyment consists in looking at Ms Hann. You would not, I think, expect to win the Miss World contest, and someone as intelligent as you would not have the slightest interest in doing so or even entering. I would hesitate even to call you conventionally beautiful. Even so you are far more attractive than most such obvious ladies and a great pleasure to look at and listen to. You have the indefinable quality that makes some ladies intensely attractive, and in short are a very dishy lady. Your intelligence is probably part of the attraction, but on the other hand I also like the close-up shots of those luscious lacquered fingernails (long may they be long!) (If that makes me kinky then that's what I am.)

Any chance of a photograph?

And one to Coronation Street's *Tracie Bennett:*

Twickenham

Dear Tracie:

May I say how lovely you look. I hope you don't mind me saying that I think you have got lovely LIPS. I do like a girl with a nicely shaped BOTTOM. I think you should win the award next year for the REAR of the YEAR!

Lots of love, Brian.

A reasonable request from an admirer of Neil Kinnock MP:

Tuffley, Gloucester
15th January 1982

Dear Mr Kinnock,

I am writing to say how much I enjoy listening to you when you take part in Robin Day's *Question Time.*

Your devastating good looks, ready wit and sense of humour fill me with admiration.

However, I cannot find it in my heart to vote for the Conservative Party or indeed the Labour Party and I am wondering if you would consider joining the Social Democrats in order that I may vote for your Party.

Television Quizmaster Hughie Green bowed out of commercial television with this call for National Moral Rearmament:

In your farewell to 1976, did you see Britain old and worn, on the brink of ruin, bankrupt in all but heritage and hope, and even those in pawn.

Where do we go from here, if time – bought with borrowed money, is lost through lack of conscience. We British, English, Scots, Welsh, Irish, who in the past earned respect throughout the world, have one more loan to come, one more transfusion for the nation that *twice* nearly bled to death for freedom, the nation that Churchill offered only blood and toil, tears and sweat. Have we really lost what he once inspired in us? The dignity of work, the urge to salvage honour. The will to win? Do we need loans for these? Folks, let us take – yes *take*, not *borrow* – this year of 1977. Let it be *our* year to lift up our heads and resolve that this time next year we can say '*We did it*, and it cost *nothing* but determination, hard work, freedom from strikes, better management and from us all *guts*!, lest without these virtues we lost our freedom for ever.'

Song

Stand up and be counted,
Take up a fighting stance.
This year of Nineteen Seventy Seven
May be our final chance.

We are still the nation
That bred the generation
Who in Nineteen Forty Dark
Made a torch from one last spark,
Fanned it into life to mark
Freedom!

It obviously struck a chord with a certain section of the viewing public. Unfortunately for Mr Green, the section did not include Thames Television's programme controller Jeremy Isaacs (now Head of Channel 4). He described it as 'toshy'. Mr and Mrs Jack Weston would not agree:

Bournemouth, Dorset
3rd January 1977

Dear Sir,

What a stupendous end Hughie Green gave to the *Opportunity Knocks* series.

By the end of his speech (monologue) my throat felt it had a tight band around it and my eyes were more than moist with tears.

My husband, a former serviceman in World War II sat absolutely motionless for more than a minute at the end.

Damned by faint praise? This was sent to Jim Slater soon after he launched his second career as childrens' author:

Dear Mr Slater,

I thank you very much for the small book that you sent me, it was a quick easy read but I quite enjoyed it.

I hope you enjoyed my book-review I sent you and I hope you write a lot more like and follow-ups to Goldenrod. I thought it might interest you to tell you that I am going to write a book.

Yours sincerely,
Kirstie Duff

This letter to Douglas Fairbanks Jr is surely all an author could desire:

January 1, 1983

Dear Mr Fairbanks,

Another new year is upon us and still no sign of your auto-biography in the bookstores. I take this opportunity to inform you of the dire consequences of delay. First of all, your many fans will stop visiting the stores and no further books will be sold. This being the case, inventories will build up causing reductions in orders to publishers and eventually the failures of both bookstores and publishers. There being no books to read, no reading will be taught. The planet will be plunged into a new DARK AGE and everyone is going to blame *you*!

When do you expect to save us from this megadisaster?

With best wishes for you
and the book,
Les A. Gladwin

And Mr Fairbanks's reply:

Dear Mr Gladwin,

In spite of all my good intentions and New Year's resolutions, I seem to be able to find many excuses to procrastinate, go slowly, revise, add or subtract more items on my book than one can imagine. My publishers have so far been wonderfully patient and tolerant with me, but I can sense their bubbling impatience in their subtle but ever polite requests that I 'Please, please, please get on with it!!'

I really and truly try and it is, I'm happy to say, progressing slowly but surely. However, I have had a full and busy life and am putting a great deal of detail of every phase of my long stay on this planet – realizing that the publishers in their 'infinite mercy and wisdom' will not hesitate to excise whatever they feel will be dull to the reader, or make the book too big and hence too expensive to produce. (Unless, of course, it comes out in several volumes!)

In any case, let me say that your New Year's letter has been a wonderfully appreciated spur, and I have sent copies to my American and British publishers in order to reassure them that there is at least one person who might buy the damn book whenever my Muse allows me to finish it. God forbid that I, like the last Roman Emperor, the second Romulus, cause a new DARK AGE and a MEGADISASTER to come about as a result of my being too dilatory. Thank you for your encouragement – I needed that.

Sincerely,

Douglas Fairbanks, Jr

Actor Peter Barkworth received these two charming letters. In each case the writer is now, alas, dead. The first is from Dame Celia Johnson and was sent in response to a fan letter which Barkworth had sent to her:

Dear Peter Barkworth,

Goodness how marvellous. Thank you very much for writing as you did – I was terribly pleased. I keep leaving your letter lying about in the hope that people will be immoral enough to read it. It seems a waste just to keep it to myself. Thank you very much.

And this was sent by Nicholas Tomalin. It refers to a documentary written by Tomalin himself, and narrated by Barkworth:

Dear Mr Barkworth,

For various reasons, complicated, political and legal, I have to keep watching that Lusitania film. By now I am bored to tears by my words but not your performance which, honestly, is bloody *marvellous*.
    Thanks.

To Peter Christie, a member of the singing group 'Instant Sunshine':

Dear Peter,

I thought your instant sunshine programme was very good. I think that if you tried very hard you could become famouse. Being quiet as you are you have a lot of time to think, so that is why I think that you write so many good songs. At school I have been working very hard. Just today I discovered that both sides of my spectacles were cracked and the glass came out. I hope you succeed in becoming famouse.

Love Rachel

To actor Jon Pertwee, 'Worzel' in the BBC Television series. The writer is a Lecturer in Psychology:

Dear Worzel,

G. K. Chesterton once wrote, as you doubtless know, 'There is a great man who makes every man feel small, but the truly great man is he who makes every man feel great.' Had it not been that Chesterton snuffed it some years prior to your appearance on the small screen, I would be of the undoubted conviction that 'the truly great man' to whom he referred was you.

But less of these sycophantic platitudes. The principal motive for my writing to you is to express my profound regret at your disappearance from Sunday afternoon viewing on LWT. You must appreciate that there now exists an uncomfortable void in my Sunday afternoons and I implore you to resume TV appearances shortly, lest I suffer the pained ravages of withdrawal. Short of TV appearances, might I advise you that my distress could, to some extent, be alleviated by the provision of a Worzel Gummidge badge or signed photograph – I will reimburse you for these and assure you that they would secure my life-long devotion to the Scarecrow cause.

As a psychologist, may I, without wishing to seem impertinent, offer some professional advice relating to your infatuation with fickle, but undeniably exquisite Aunt Sally? Tell her to bugger off! I appreciate that the short-term consequences will be unbearable in the extreme but urge you to think of the long-term benefits of such action – assuming you haven't disintegrated or been burned by then.

Again oh dilapidated one! a hasty return to your rightful place. MY TELEVISION ON SUNDAY AFTERNOONS!

*To April Ashley from Able Seamen Grimwood, Gwent, Shep-
pard. A few years before April had been an Able Seaman
herself:*

Dear Miss Ashley,

It is with hearts full of hope that we write this our first letter to
you, an ex-mariner but now a beautiful woman.

In our mess deck we have forty-one pin-ups of various
young, good-looking women, but nowhere among these can
be found one such as you. We would willingly tear these
down if we could replace them with portraits of yourself. We
have collected almost all of the paper clippings of you but
these are not sufficient and do not do justice to your beautiful
self.

We humbly beseech you to grant us our wish as yours was
granted early on that eventful morning in May, two years ago.
Since then you have climbed to the top of the beauty tree and
there you will always stay.

If our wish cannot be granted we will be the most unhappy
men in the world.

Yours hopefully,
David, Arthur and John

PS Please reply, if only to say no.

My first fan letter arrived the day after I blushed and stumbled through my first television news broadcast. 'Dear Miss Carper,' it said, 'Why don't you Piss Off?' It wasn't signed. Most of the sort aren't. But whoever wrote it would have been satisfied by its effect. At that moment I'd willingly have pissed off anywhere that offered immediate and permanent obscurity and, years later, I remember that brief and careless message better than thousands of kind and encouraging letters I've received since.

Abusive mail is horribly memorable and cruelly wounding. At first. After a while you get a taste for them: the rather wildly addressed envelope . . . the coloured ink . . . the curious use of capitals and underlinings. You start to look forward to them . . . and if you get as many as me you end up a connoisseur.

The classic hate-letter is anonymous. The few that give a name and address also give their victims the chance of revenge. Quentin Crisp offers appointments to the (numerous) twisted people who threaten to kill him. Jilly Cooper replies along the lines: 'Thank you for your interesting letter. Constructive criticism is always welcome, particularly from perceptive and informed readers . . .' *then changes the addressee's sex by substituting Miss for Mr and vice versa.*

Neil Kinnock MP sends a standard letter to excessively abusive correspondents:

House of Commons
London SW1A 0AA

Dear Sir/Madam,

I think that you should be made aware that some poor soul who is clearly unbalanced is using your name and address in letters to Members of Parliament, including myself.

If you have any more trouble of this nature, please let me know and I will bring it to the attention of the appropriate authorities.

Yours sincerely,
Neil Kinnock

This one, to Neil Kinnock, was painstakingly written in capital letters . . . no name.

OUR GRANFER SAYS YOUR OLD MAN HAD NO NEED TO WORK 7 DAYS A WEEK AS YOU SAID IN THE PAPER. HE WAS GREEDY FOR MONEY LIKE YOU. HE SAY YOU HAVE NOT DONE A USEFUL DAY'S WORK – HE SAY YOU ARE LIKE MOST LABOUR MP SPIVS ON THE WORKERS BACKS. THATS WHY OUR GRANFER DO NOT VOTE LABOUR HE SAY WORKERS ARE MADE JO SOAPS BY PEOPLE WHO MAKE A FAT LIVING FROM RUNNING UNIONS AND LABOUR PARTY.

GRANFER LIVED IN BEDWELLY. HE KNEW WHERE YOU LIVED. HE SAY YOU WORSHIP MAMMON. I GO TO CHAPEL. I WORSHIP GOD. SIR GAVE ME THIS PAPER TO WRITE FOR GRANFER. SIR IS MY TEACHER.

An ominous fan letter to Sarah Lucas of Capital Radio:

Dear Sarah,

What do you mean you won't marry me? I can tell you're really coming round to the idea, despite what you say, so I have taken the liberty of booking Guildford Cathedral for the afternoon of July 3rd – kick-off 1.30 pm – for our wedding. I know it's not Westminster Abbey or St Paul's, but at least it's a Cathedral and it's next door to me, too. I'll await your confirmation of our wedding plans. Meanwhile if you get time to come down to Guildford for a pint of best bitter and a jam sandwich all the better.

My own favourite abusive letter is this – from a regular:

Carter Why Don't you pack up you're a proper Bore and I think you are slightly unbalanced Your grinning face spoils the News which we have already heard 3 or 4 times before. It seems to me that you are a bit Loose up Top. So do us a favour and pack up.

To Sandor Eles of Crossroads. This letter is suspiciously similar to the previous one, sent to me — same rather wild scrawl and arbitrary use of capitals, with the final few words erupting into larger and paper-piercingly fierce script:

Sandor Eles Your a Bigheaded
Deceitfull Conceited BASTARD
the trouble with you, you
Cannot Leave women Alone.
You a manager? of what, Your a
greasy Skunk
Your not fit to be where
there are Women
Your a sex maniac
Such persons should be Led
round the streets Like a Stalion
as You are
Do us all a favour and
GET OUT YOU BASTARD

My colleague at Thames Television, Geoffrey Hayes, the pre-senter of the children's programme Rainbow, *received this one. It was signed 'Unadmirer' — as though he couldn't guess!*

Liverpool

Geoffrey,

Get your stupid ugly mug off the screen or are you really as demented as you seem? And I'd like to ram an apple down that stupid bungler gob.

Give up your stupid laugh.

Can't a 14 year old see something good when she comes home for dinner? BUGGER OFF!!

Same idea – different fruit! – to Acker Bilk:

Edinburgh

I listened to your broadcast on Sunday night when you murdered the beautiful waltz 'Always'. You should get the rough end of a pineapple up your arse, you bastard.

Acker Bilk later wrote this to a friend:

. . . I met the Queen on Monday night and she asked me if I had received the letter from her old man! He's sending a whole case of pineapples . . .'

*This was sent to show-jumping commentator Dorian Williams
– it's odious both for comparisons, and ingredients!*

Cocktail Racing

1 large tablespoon of Epsom Salts
4 Cascara tablets
1 bar Exlax chocolate

Method

Crush all ingredients and mix with hot water. Give to
Raymond Brooks-Ward 1 hour before every show. Put re-
serve notice on loo.

Viewers will be spared having to listen to his awful voice.
He may get carried away with the excitement but why should
we have to suffer.

Dorian Williams has a pleasing and pleasant voice but
please spare us the constant repetitions of pedigrees of both
horses and riders. Suggest time saved be used to study
French. Excruciating pronunciation is worse than toothache
but we like him. Tell David Vine to open his mouth and not
speak through clenched teeth.

And this was sent, anonymously, from Australia, to the actor Robin Bailey when it was announced that he was to go there to play Professor Higgins in a production of My Fair Lady:

So you are to play Professor Higgins out here! Trust the 'firm' to make a squint-eyed choice like that! Why can't we have Max Oldaker, and then we'd have impeccable diction, some charm, and a voice – all of which you lack.

I haven't forgotten your Shakespearian crucifixion in this country – your hoodlum Grafiano – your vulgar Lucio – oh well at best we'll be spared your wearing tights you don't know how to hitch up properly – and a repulsive codpiece!

So you are to crucify Shaw, too? Daresay Higgins will have some 'sex' for the first time. Why don't you copy Presley and play the part with an embroidered fly? Do anything to distract from your putrid voice, face and personality!

If you are an indication of what we're to expect in the casting God help poor Eliza!

Daresay you're coming out for peanuts however. That's all you're worth.

Sports commentator Peter West got this at a time when he was appearing regularly in an advertisement for frozen peas:

Dear Blockhead,

How does it feel eating your words? As you said on TV 'The Ashes are in the bag for England.' A word of advice: never count your chickens until they are hatched.

You stick to advertising Birds Eye Peas. They are full of wind, too.

Another one to Peter West. This from a former professional player:

Northampton

Dear Sir,

Please break yourselves of the habit of talking about a ball bowled as 'a delivery'. Women have 'deliveries', bowlers have 'balls' – Instead of saying 'That was a good delivery' – why not say 'That was a good ball'? And who are 'The Cricketing Gods'?

You may know the story of the argument between God and the Devil as to who would win a match between their two sides – God said he would – He had W.G., Jack Hobbs, and many more – 'Ah' said the Devil – 'But, you see, I've got all the Umpires.'

To Radio 3 announcer Tom Crowe:

Liverpool
6.1.75

Dear Mr Crowe,

I had hoped that with the turn of the year you would reform. But you are still con-*sher*ting as badly as ever around the landscape. I wonder whether the lapse is due to ignorance, tone-deafness, or bloody-mindedness? It *could* be ignorance, because a constant listener to BBC radio is lucky if he doesn't hear at least ten examples of mispronunciation, wrongly placed accents or meaningless emphasis every day.

It *could* be tone deafness. Perhaps you think you are really saying 'conchairto'.

But I think the most probable explanation is bloody-mindedness. 'To hell with it! If I want to say "consherto" I bloody well will!'

PS I sincerely hope that you will never have to utter over the radio the word CHIT. I think we all know what would happen.

To Jean Rook, assistant editor of the Daily Express, *in response to a particularly spicy article:*

Bearsden
Glasgow
24th March 1982

Dear Madam,

Despite some very confused thinking on your part, especially on morals, ethics etc., and which is evident in your articles, you are in a very privileged and responsible position.

I say to you in the name of the Lord – Do not abuse your position to excite your own vanity. Find out what is the truth on lawful and spiritual matters before you launch into foolishness.

The Bible says, 'He who is often reproved, yet stiffens his neck will suddenly be broken beyond healing.' Prov 21:1 and 'A scoffer seeks wisdom in vain, but knowledge is easy for a man of understanding.' 'Leave the presence of a fool for there you do not meet words of knowledge.' Prov. 14:6,7 'The fool says in his heart, there is no God.' Psalm 14:1

I challenge you to read I Corinthians Ch. 2 thoughtfully, and if you are so inclined, to answer this letter truthfully. You will know then how good your articles really are, in your heart.

---

and her reply:

Dear Mr Baldwin,

Thank you for your Bible lesson. I am quite conversant with the Book.

Yours sincerely,
Jean Rook
Assistant Editor

One from the archives. This was sent to the Daily Telegraph *in 1956. The correspondent referred to is Jim Swanton!*

> Stanmore, Middx
> July 1956
>
> Dear Sir,
>
> Don't you think the time has come for your cricket correspon-dent to be quietly disposed of: stuffed, and placed in the Long Room with the curved bats, the sparrow, and other freaks of the noble game?
>
> L T Sainsbury

Ten years later, Mr Swanton received this:

> Howick,
> Auckland NZ
> Dear Mr Swanton,
>
> I emigrated to New Zealand in 1957 and recently acquired a paperback copy of your excellent book *Sort of a Cricket Person*. I was amazed to see a letter quoted on page 286, written by me in 1956 and addressed to the Editor of the *Daily Telegraph*. I would like to assure you that it was meant to be witty but in cold print I realise it could well be offensive.
>
> I would like to assure you that no offence was intended at the time and would appreciate your assurance that none was taken.

Mr Sainsbury is not the only person to write in haste and repent. Broadcaster Nigel Rees received this, in 1977:

Dear Mr Rees,

I am writing to say how sorry I am to hear you taking part in such a beastly programme as *The Burkiss Way*. I put the radio on expecting to get the news. I had to listen to a silly disgusting entertainment – it was unfortunate for me, I was unable to reach the 'off' switch. The crudeness was bad enough. You might at least have had the decency to leave the Bible out of it.

I always look forward to hearing you and Brian Redhead but that half hour made me feel sick and my head has ached ever since . . .

Mrs E. Coleman

Two years later, he got this:

Dear Mr Rees,

I am taking this opportunity to write and apologise for my letter sent some time ago. It was very unfortunate that your name was the only one I knew on that programme. I had listened to you and Mr Redhead with particular pleasure and could not associate you with such a stupid programme as *The Burkiss Way.* Being an impulsive person I sat down at once and wrote that letter. I've since regretted that letter and wished to write, thinking only of the nicer side of you.

Although I'm a very old woman and partially blind, I am still a very intelligent person with a sense of humour and an excellent memory. Even now I can enjoy a good laugh (I am 96 years). I also enjoy horse-racing and occasionally place a bet. I spend a lot of time listening to the radio and am lucky to have a blind radio with ear-phones so I'm never lonely. I often wake up and listen in about 3 a.m. I hear world news and do a great deal of writing and in the last few months have just finished a novel. I've written and sent other pieces to publishers but this is the first novel I've tried. It has 74,000 words. Rejections do not perturb me. I have a friend who untangles and types what I do. A newphew does research and helps get everything in order for me.

Being in an old people's home is not the best way to end one's life. Most of the 415 people here are in their 80s and 90s. One is easily bored. This is a very modern home with a fine matron who escaped from Estonia. We are lucky to have her. She is adored by staff and residents.

I heard you today telling how many insulting letters you receive. That's too bad. I regret mine. It wasn't meant to be personal and I hope I may hear you again. So far I've only heard you on *Quote–Unquote*. Old age is very frustrating, especially when you have to depend on others.

Jessica Mitford, author of (among other things) The American Way of Death, *a damning indictment of the American exploitation of death, recently gave a short interview to a newspaper describing how she and her husband, Bob Treuhaft, came to meet. The interview appeared like this:*

Writer Jessica Mitford and lawyer Bob Treuhaft met in the cafeteria line at the Office of Price Administration, a World War II agency in Washington DC. Mitford says: 'Bob was a lawyer and my title was "sub-eligible typist", for which I was paid $1440 a year. What I'd do,' she said, 'was to sort of eat everything as I went along. The line moved slowly and there was a handy shelf underneath where, after polishing off their contents, I deposited the empty containers. I'd end up at the cashier with one coffee: 5 cents. Bob, on observing this, found it terribly frugal and he asked me out. He was engaged to some other people at the time – he was constantly proposing you see. Eventually he married me.'

Ms Mitford received a photostat of this newspaper cutting with a rubber-stamped 'ABSOLUTELY DISGRACEFUL' across it. It was accompanied by this letter:

It's absolutely reprehensible that a person who advocates and complains about undertakers 'Taking people' in overcharging death costs would herself be an out-and-out thief! What an indictment! Suppose every customer did the same? And then have the audacity to publish what a cute trick it was to snag an admiring husband-to-be! By being a THIEF! You both should be ashamed of yourselves. It wouldn't be so bad if you didn't both set yourselves up as being Saviours of Mankind. At a large group gathering the above topic revolted all of us. I suppose the above tactics are helpful to a law profession. To be sneaky and dishonest!

Some constructive advice to me, from a viewer:

London N1
26th July, 1982

Dear Miss Carter,

I am getting very weary of watching the top of your head while you try to read the news and get dizzy with the constant bobbing up and down. Why can't you keep your head still?? Why do you not have an idiot board or more aptly a board for an idiot? Why should viewers have to put up with broadcasters who cannot even read what is written down for them correctly. Do try and improve, dear.

This was sent to London Weekend Television presenter Fred Housego:

Attention of George (sic) Housego

Sir,

I told my family at the time of *Mastermind* that yours was a 'surface knowledge', adding that the moment you were exposed to real competition your number would be up. Trouble from the viewers point of view is that we are now lumbered with another 'personality'. That you have never heard of, or know about, the work of the Great Masters. Never sat at the feet of the Gallileos, Michael Angelos, Confucious, matters nothing. Give 'em some cockney froth, you'll get by. Personally, though, I think you're the luckiest man alive to get by by a whisker, as you do.

To the producer of BBC Radio 4's Start the Week:

Dear Sir,

There was a time when it was a pleasure to listen to *Start the Week with Richard Baker.* However, nearly every time I dare to switch on these past few months I am amazed to hear Fred Housego. Why? Richard Baker does not need any assistance from a member of the public, least of all from one with an unpleasing voice, no personality and a lamentably poor command of English which necessitates the use of such meaningless words as 'bloody'.

When I saw Mr Housego come bottom in *Mastermind International* last week I heaved a sigh of relief, thinking that surely that would be the last we should hear of him, but alas, there he was again, causing many others as well as myself to cringe and wonder – why? It couldn't be that he was already billed in *Radio Times* as this week's edition as a depleted one, so I have come to the conclusion that the only possible reason for Fred Housego's repeated appearances is that he has some sort of blackmail hold on someone at the BBC. I have tried, but can think of no sound reason for his inclusion. All I can hope is that his contract will soon come to an end.

And a little something to ruffle the rural feathers in Ambridge; this was sent to the Eddie Grundy Fan Club (Grundy is the baddie of the Archers):

Sir,

I've been writing to the Archers for years, suggesting useful modifications like wiping them out in 'plane crashes, farming accidents etc. until in the end it could be called the Grundies. However, they haven't taken my advice. I thought they *could* have got rid of that unspeakable slug Tom Forrest by Alan (psychopathic killer) Frazer. But alas they didn't. Do you have any other ideas?

This was sent to Shaw Taylor, presenter of Police 5:

To Shaw Taylor,

I think you are disgusting. You wear such bloody wide ties and have you ever heard of a little invention called 'Topex' by any chance?

I bet your mummy gets your suits for you from Brentford Nylons – you're the only one that keeps them in business.

Oh go and pick your nose or your arse as the case may be – nylon underpants are *very* uncomfortable. I wish someone would lose you and forget to take down your registration number.

Yours,
Mr Comfortable
in cotton underpants from Marks and Sparks.

A gentleman from Fife sent this to Nigel Rees. Clearly, he is Not Amused:

St. Andrew's, Fife
5th February 1976

Dear Mr Rees,

Your programme *Quote . . . Unquote* is one of the wittiest on radio at this time but it would be even better if you could eliminate the slightly vulgar elements. I don't think I'm particularly puritanical but the people who listen to Radio 4 are pretty square and it is too cold up here to have much of a permissive society.

Last week I think you mentioned Antonia Fraser; I haven't the faintest idea what she gets up to but the remark was in bad taste. It would be different if she had been dead 200 years. This letter needs no reply.

And Nor is He:

Brighton, Sussex
11th September 1979

Dear Friend,

I like your programme *Quote–Unquote* but I am constrained to warn you that your sarcastic and caustic remarks on biblical subjects ill become you, and these are heard by God and HE is not mocked (Galatians 6.7). I'm truly sorry that such a nice person as you seem to be should take this risk – the ultimate consequences of which you must be wholly unaware.

Best wishes.

The wife of the Minister of Pawling Independent Baptist Church in Phoenixville, Arizona, was certainly not tickled by Raymond Briggs's Santa *book:*

9th December, 1975

Dear Mr Briggs,

My six year old son chose the following book from the public library, as it was on special display and featured as a Notable Children's Book.

To my dismay when reading him the story I was upset to see one of the pictures portraying Santa performing an act of personal hygiene. Also the notations indicating that he cursed. The entire story is negative and very depressing. I am truly sorry this book is on the market, and I would recommend you to read some of Dr Maltz's books on Positive Approach to Life.

You definitely owe an apology to all children who read this book and I am saying this in love. I pray that God would change your heart and that you will be remembered by all children as an author who brings delight and moral standards to all who read your books.

May you have a happy Christmas, forgive me if I have spoiled it for you.

To Jilly Cooper, after a television appearance. This was actually signed 'Definitely Disgusted'!

Dear Miss Cooper,

Having waded through a bit of the utter balderdash in the MAIL I would suggest after seeing you on TV, that you're eligible to be included in the 'Great Unwashed'.

You looked (and sounded, when you managed about two intelligible comments) as though you were drunk or on drugs.

Try combing your mane once in a while, or don't they sell combs in Putney? It would be an improvement if you covered all your face instead of half your face and one eye!

To Janet Street-Porter:

Dear Janet,

As a regular viewer of your programme, I would like to comment on your appearance. Firstly, your teeth are disgraceful. Who is your dentist? The way you talk it's like as if you had a *hot* potato in your mouth and your glasses I just can't describe. Apart from all that you seem to be a kind-hearted person and a good giggler.

As for Fred Housego he thinks he's it but Michael Aspel is alright I suppose.

Pamela aged 11.

Rather a puzzling one, to Jean Rook, who is actually quite well-known for being rude about the Royals:

London, E17
22nd May 1981

To Jean Rook,

I do not usually read your scribblings because they make me feel sick, but whenever I do read them you are sycophantically eulogising about royalty.

It is paradoxical that a country which calls itself a democracy should also retain hereditary privilege. I suppose you are more to be pitied than blamed for your boot-licking attitude as it is probably a congenital defect.

To Lucinda Green (Prior-Palmer):

Littlemore
Oxford

Dear Madam,

Recently I obtained your book *Up, Up and Away* from the Library. I was reading it with much pleasure until I came to page 204 and read 'it reminds me of a poof at a hairdresser'.

Then I stopped reading and threw the book away. What a dreadful expression to use.

I thought you were someone to admire. Now I know you are not.

To William Donaldson, creator of Henry Root, from the York University Literary Watchdog committee:

Dear Sir,

We have come into possession of your recently published book *The Further Letters of Henry Root*. After much discussion of its contents we have decided that the only course of action open to us is to write directly to you in order to voice our protests against the narrow-minded, bigoted attitude of the character you have created as the author of various letters which make up the bulk of the publication.

You, like ourselves, judging from the severely ironic tone of some of your letters, have obvious left-wing sympathies. However, your book contains such disgustingly sexist, racist and reactionary overtones that there can be no justification for its publication, even as a means of poking fun at the establishment.

In the ideal socialist system, as you no doubt understand, such ideology as that of Henry Root would be punishable. Unless you can justify to us the appalling liberties that you have taken with the mind of the working man we will not cease in our efforts to have this book banned and will embark on a strong campaign of counter publicity to see that this unwitting fascist propaganda does not find its way on to our campus.

Two more people who didn't appreciate Henry Root:

Dear Sir,

May I say that on reading your TWO books, *The Letters of Henry Root* and *The Further Letters of Henry Root* (lent to me by a Tory friend) that I feel that it is this type of literature that is responsible for the general lack of manners in the young today. The young today seem to feel that to be rude is to be clever and your books would seem to give support to this type of feeling.

I would encourage anyone with a genuine grievance to complain, but to waste people's time on what can only be considered as commercial rudeness I find deplorable.

Sir,

Your puerile scrawlings in your alleged letters would seem to indicate that you possess a snide, sniggering juvenile and immature sense of humour. Indeed you would seem to gain gratification by lampooning many people and institutions who have done far more to deserve public acclaim than you would hope to do in your entire life! If I had you in my battery, I would see to it that you doubled round the parade ground until every last vestige of that stupid smirk was wiped off your sniggering face permanently! *And* you would have to do it in Full Service Marching Order.

Unfortunately, thanks to the influence of lazy, scrounging, idle, shiftless, gutless Bolsheviks like yourself, National Service is a thing of the past – an occurrence which I am convinced, has done more to destroy the standing of our great nation in the eyes of the world than all the social security handouts (which I'm sure are your main source of income apart from the ill-gotten gains of your *disgusting* little book).

To Larry Adler:

Mr Adler,

After reading your latest eating out column in the give away magazine *Portrait*, August issue, the time has come after long suffering, to tell you how much of a disservice you are doing to catering and British eating-out in general.

Do please tell me, have you ever eaten a GOOD simple lunch or dinner in your life that you have ever paid for out of your own pocket?

We all need to work hard to earn a living but it appears that all *you* need to do is wiggle a silly tongue and pen.

This letter was sent to Bob Wellings during an anti-smoking campaign waged by BBC's Nationwide *programme. In it all the presenters, including Bob, publicly, and – he admits now – perhaps a little self-righteously, gave up the weed in an effort to lead their millions of viewers along the same path of self-improvement. This viewer, however, wasn't to be led:*

Dear Whellin,

I'm so fed up with you self-satisfied lot and your giving up smoking. I'm 68 years of age. . . . I've never had a cigarette in my life nor have I ever wanted to. But you lot have so got up my left nostril that I'm writing to give notice that I'm hereby taking up smoking from next Tuesday.

I gave up smoking myself about three years ago – though I wasn't so rash as to announce it on television (given the relapses I suffered en route to a fag-free life it's just as well). So this post-card, sent to me very recently, is something of a puzzle:

TO FAG-ASH LIL (ALIAS RITA)

WHEN ARE YOU GOING TO STOP EATING CIGARETTES AND READ THE NEWS INSTEAD OF EATING THESE GAS-PERS AND *GASPING OUT THE NEWS* READ IT, RITA – CUT OUT THE FAGS (PHEW)

The card was addressed: 'FIRST CLASS POST TO SECOND CLASS READER.'

To Stirling Moss, after he wrote a report of a test drive on the ARA 2000 sports car:

---

68 Parkhill Road
London NW3

Dear Stirling Moss,

Cars are your life. They are the curse of my life. The motorist in Britain (and no doubt elsewhere) has it all his/her own way. Oh yes, they have to pay for it. And why not? Cars are despicable, dangerous, destructive, tyrannical, expensive and pullutant; let their owners pay up.

The money spent on buying the ARA 2000 if spent on improving the mind of the buyer would help to change him/her from being a selfish ignorant buffoon to a humane, learned, thinking human. I see ignorant, dull, aggressive men smashing their way through our streets daily in vastly expensive vehicles whilst the finer things of life receive infinitely less financial support than the wheels of these same vehicles.

As for driving hard and quickly I can tell you this that motorists drive hard and quickly down our road often exceeding speed limits and generally behaving in an anti-social manner. The police do nothing. My wife says she'd like to drive an ARA 2000 right up your arse. I agree with her.

Bernard Kelly.

And his reply:

London
20th September 1979

Dear Mr Kelly,

Thank you for your letter which arrived whilst I was in Italy watching quite a few maniacs entertaining 150,000 people.

Actually, I would like to congratulate you on writing such an amusing and stupid letter. I am really impressed that you included your name and address, because usually one does not get the opportunity of answering this sort of drivel. I regret to say that I haven't got the time to contest all your nonsensical observations, but hopefully you will give a little bit of thought to the many thousands of people that use the internal combustion engines to help their fellow man, whether by driving an ambulance, taking urgently needed supplies to Cambodia, or just 'wasting their time' helping an unfortunate lady with a difficult birth.

I close sending my best wishes, and hope that you will use your energies to assist people, rather than destroy them.

Yours truly,
Stirling Moss

This letter was sent to Mary O'Hara, together with her hand-bag, which she had left in a London cab:

13th November, 1978

Dear Mary,

Don't panic. Here is your handbag back with all its contents intact. I picked it up in a cab I used on Friday afternoon. I could have done a lot of damage to your bank account but I didn't. However, as a small reward and to teach you a big lesson in being more careful in future, I awarded myself £50 from your Access card. I feel this is a nominal charge for returning your property.

A well-wisher

XX

And this one was also sent to Mary O'Hara after she had sung 'When I'm 64' on the radio:

Dear Miss O'Hara,

I was half asleep when your programme on Sunday December 10 was ending. But I did hear you play that terrifying record 'When I'm 64.' Nothing annoys me more than to be reminded that I'm getting older. Not a day goes by without someone on the radio making some remark to remind us that we are getting older.

Curse you for playing that bloody record! When my birthday comes round I curse the bloody day and if anyone sent me a birthday card I would kick them. That is how much it annoys me.

To *The King Singers (Alastair Hume), after their appearance at the Royal Command Performance, 1978:*

Nottingham
14th November, 1978

Sirs,

I was enjoying the Royal Variety Performance very much until you came on the stage singing your silly song slandering various nations.

As a Welshwoman I strongly object to your calling the Welsh dishonest etc. I was too annoyed to listen further, so what you said after that I don't know.

I'd prefer to be called mean as you called the Scots (what an insult to the Queen Mother) rather than dishonest. As a very honest person I take exception to this stupid and humiliating song which was listened to by millions last night.

Please don't sing it again, destroy it, and stop trying to be clever and funny at other people's expense.

This came from a television viewer, and was sent to Richard Stilgoe when he first presented the consumer slot on BBC Television's Nationwide:

Whiteparish Salisbury
Wilts
7th December 1973

Dear Sir or Madam,

You have ruined a very good programme on *Nationwide* by bringing in that *clown* to help Val who did a very good job on her own. For one thing he insists on saying 'p' instead of pence and his character does not suit the programme. It is a serious programme and should not be treated as a joke such as he is doing.

Please get rid of him or at least keep him out of sight and return to the old style of showing this programme which is a well worthy one and commendable.

More pitfalls for broadcasters. This was sent to golfing commentator Peter Allis:

Dear Mr Alliss,

I always enjoy your commentaries immensely but may I ask for one small favour? As you take so much care to get the young Spaniard's name right could you please do the same for the young German. It should be Bairnheart Lung – as in 'lung' – er. BBC's German service will confirm it. After all, they wouldn't dream of calling you Peter Ullis!

There's nothing like the subject of animals – and in particular animal experiments – to bring the British to the boil. Dr Rob Buckman received this vitriolic missive from a no-doubt usually kindly soul, after he wrote an article in TV Times *suggesting that some animal experiments may be justified:*

Dear Dr Buckman,

After reading your opinion in the last copy of *TV Times* regarding animal research I do not agree with you at all. There is no need to think about it as you suggested as I am completely against it and so is my husband who is blind but would not wish any animal of any description to be tortured to enable him to get his sight back. And he has not been wearing mascara either. You are an animal murderer, may God forgive you. I will never watch *Where There's Life* again and I shall never feel the same about you. It just shows how mistaken you can be about someone. I'm the owner of three sweet, adorable chihuahas and I can tell you you won't get your hands on them – that's for sure.

*There are a lot of dotty people about. Cheerfully, harmlessly,
charmingly dotty. For a start there's a surprisingly large number of people who think television viewing is a two-way
exercise. Robert Dougall recalls a letter from a woman in
Scotland who lived with her mother in a one-roomed crofter's
cottage. Come nine o'clock and it was time for Grannie to get
ready for bed. At the same time, Dougall appeared on BBC
Television to read the news. The writer was puzzled as to why
her mother always went through an elaborate modesty routine,
tugging her nightie across her chest and sometimes even ret-
iring behind the furniture. It seemed strange, she wrote, as the
nearest neighbours were some forty miles away. One night she
asked her mother outright. With a suspicious glance at the
television screen Grannie explained: 'I dinna want him tae see
me like this . . .'*

*Another letter sent to Robert Dougall tells of an old lady
who took great care when she returned home after drawing her
pension, to hide it away in an old tobacco jar on the mantel-
piece. Before she stowed it away she always took a tablecloth
from the drawer and used it to cover the television screen. 'Just
in case!'*

*Andrew Gardner and Reginald Bosanquet worked together
at ITN – for years the country's best-known and most popular
newsreading duo. At the end of each programme, after the
Goodnight, the microphones were faded and, as the credits
rolled, the camera drew back to reveal the two apparently
exchanging pleasantries as they gathered up their papers.*

Hundreds of people wrote in and asked them what they were saying to each other. But one woman already knew:

She wrote:

Please send me ONE MILLION POUNDS damages by return of post. This for watching me get undressed for bed last night.

PS And don't think I don't know what you were saying to each other afterwards, either . . .

Here's somebody else who can spot a conspiracy when he sees one. It was sent in 1973, to Sir Geoffrey Howe, then Minister for Consumer Affairs:

Dear Sir,

Hitler cut four inches off the German's shirt tails and their people froze and lost their war. But much more has been cut off the shirt tails in the UK. Is this international economic sabotage during a fuel crisis?

   A young salesman in Simpson in the West End tried to sell me an evening shirt for £9.50 with mini length tails. I protested and his reply was that is what people want. This I did not accept, there have been many public opinion polls but none on the length of shirt tails. It was and is a case of giving short measure and this is cheating on a national scale.

   I hope you will look into the matter.

This was sent to Yehudi Menuhin from The Kingdom of Heaven. On closer scrutiny it appeared this was situated somewhere in Calcutta. It included a photograph of the risen Christ complete with his wife and kiddies:

My dear Maestro,

Greetings and Shalom from the Lord! It is his pleasure to inform you that the once-crucified fingers play delightful music, as if Bach and Beethoven playing the Indian Ragas on the piano and the violin and his son, the Living Mozart accompanying him on the piano with grace and finesse that only heaven can provide.

The Lord would be pleased to contribute his gift to the Amnesty International through his art and music and he hopes a gramophone recording will come forward to market a few discs for this purpose. The Lord will be a man of 76 winters on 27th November 1980. But he is quite able to perform his music for 2 or 3 hours at one sitting and he works the whole day on his art and calligraphy on Biblical subjects which will have a ready market in the world after this Christmas.

If these ideas appeal to you we can join together and perform miracles to save the world.

Yours truthfully,
Jesus Christ
(New name Annada Munsi,
according to Revelation 3:12)

And from the other camp . . . This was sent to Thames Television.

Sir,

Due to certain circumstances some years ago my brain was removed and I died. The surgeon who performed the operation could not believe it when I returned to life some years later – still in possession of all my faculties, and animated by Satan! Previously I had been very religious and been to Hell and back several times. Satan gave me youth, health and happiness. I have given Him my Life and He works through me. In this way I can heal or destroy. The 'God' everyone else worships evolved from an ancient Hebrew tribal God, a myth called 'Yahweh', and is non-existent. Unfortunately the talents with which Satan has endowed me are not appreciated by the aggressive and uncouth types who slouch around today. My operatic singing and classical violin playing have been received with gross contempt and indifference by 'rock' addicts – and yet if I were to ask these indolent creatures why they exist, they would be totally unable to reply. But my Master has told me why *I* exist and what I must do for Him!

One of the things the writer was commanded to do, the letter continued, was to crash a Boeing 747 on Thames Television. At the time of writing, this has not come to pass.

To Harry Greenway MP:

Dear Sir,   27th July 1982

THE UNION JACK

I listened with interest when you were interviewed on 29th June 1982 on LBC Radio with regard to the 'dirty, frayed and frequently upside-down' flag flying over Parliament.

I often visit Westminster on business and must say that although I frequently gaze upon the Parliamentary buildings, I cannot recall that I have ever noticed the Union flag to be any of the things you have suggested. Even if it were, could not the following interpretation be placed upon it?

DIRTY – In spite of the marks of assault upon our great country, the mud-slinging of disagreeable foreign powers and the smears of repellent dissidents, the Union standard still flutters unashamedly at the mast.

FRAYED – The web of strands from the fraying edge surely symbolises the standards of the British way of life ebbing out to the world and, as in the Empire days, bringing democracy, enlightenment and, in many cases, liberation.

UPSIDE-DOWN – This is obvious. From ANY angle, Britain is really GREAT. From Port Stanley to Dresden, from the Crusades to Aden, the British have shown tolerance, understanding and reason. British trade unions, from Grunwick to the NHS, from the mines to the Railways have shown they are strong and represent fully the rights of the workers. In much the same way British forces recently showed the world that even a small group of sheep-farmers 8000 miles away and already excluded from British residence could rely on support from our armies.

Sir, a clean, upright flag in good repair flying over Westminster would not symbolically convey that which I have outlined. Keep it dirty, frayed and often upturned in the call of the common man!

I look forward to hearing of your observations on the matter.   Yours faithfully,

To April Ashley:

> Weston-super-Mare,
> 29th July 1962
>
> Dear April,
>
> I am keeping a dossier of your life history and events as clipped from the above paper, and a short time ago I wrote you a special letter care of that paper in which I proposed you should ally yourself to me in the space act that I have now printed as per enclosed leaflet. I sent a photograph of myself but up to the time of writing this second letter I have had no reply from you.
>
> Yet again you visited rather a common type of club recently here in Weston and I thought at the time you might have looked me up in view of my letter, but alas I did not see you.
>
> You are having a very hectic and certainly not happy time according to the papers, and this morning I was very satisfied to read that you had broken with Hon Arthur Corbett which to my character reading of you both is for the best.
>
> I don't usually write to strange women like I have to you, especially as I am a bachelor and have never so far associated with any member of the opposite sex. You will see therefore that something quite out of the ordinary has occurred now between us to urge me to write in such a manner to you.
>
> Now will you read my leaflet carefully through as it is the most amazing thing that I have ever experienced in all my life, and it is a forerunner to yet a still more amazing possibility.
>
> I refer to the possibility of a return trip to the planet Venus which I am awaiting every day, and in the event of your teaming up with me, *I could take you as the first woman on earth to ever visit the planet with me as well.*
>
> Now please don't take this offer as a fantastic and an utter impossibility, as already I have had a man in this office for one

hour, who was picked up by the Venusians in Los Angeles, California, in a flying saucer, landed on a huge space ship larger than the liner *Queen Elizabeth* and brought back to this Earth again round the other side of the moon that we never see from this world.

I am now booked up too on both sound and television broadcasting and have been seen on Westward Television with my first partner, who being a married lady, found the tie too much, hence I am now seeking a second partner, who I name 'Venusia' to carry on with.

Please reply to let me know when you can commence work with me.

To Duncan Fallowell, April Ashly's biographer:

Dear Mr Fallowell,

I recently read something you wrote in *Boulevard* magazine, I think, in which you said 'those who lose their innocence at an early age, never lose it entirely', and said how important it was for people to be corrupted from time to time. I agree. I am nearly 19 and have been trying to get corrupted for ages – if I came down to London, would you help me? I don't just mean going with girls or boys, that's easy, but really letting something else get to you.

That's what you meant isn't it? This letter's a warning really – I live at home and can't put my address on it. Don't be surprised if you hear from me again in a few weeks. You can always tell me to piss off again.

Is this what's meant by character building? From a Gordon-stoun prep school master, to Richard Mabey, author of Food for Free:

Gordonstoun Preparatory School
Banffshire, Scotland
12th July 1977

Dear Mr Mabey,

We have just returned from our 'survival' expedition to Cape Wrath and amongst our other unusual food items we ate considerable numbers of the large seashore woodlouse, *Lvgia oceanica.* They are I suppose an acquired taste, but not one of our party disliked them! If anything they are slightly reminiscent of shrimp when boiled. Surprisingly, maybe, they do not turn pink when boiled. We can wholeheartedly recommend them and we ate them whenever and wherever we found large populations of them. We will look forward to your next edition of *Food for Free* – maybe with Lvgia added?

We also ate Common Toad (rather tough and stringy but quite wholesome), Common Frog where these were very numerous (very tasty indeed – a very popular dish), Common Gull (very dark meat with a strongish flavour, but very edible when spit roasted). Sticklebacks (fried like whitebait – one group ate 71 at one sitting), as well as several of the more unusual items described in your book. (Also Shore Crabs – very nice indeed.)

Dear Sir,

With reference to the travel article in today's *Sunday Telegraph* magazine by the Hon Nicholas Monson, we would like to point out that despite his dilettantish approach to camping in that article, the Hon Nick is not such a stranger to the joys of holidays under canvas as he would have you believe.

We wonder if he remembers a windswept, rain-sodden fortnight in Cornwall in the summer of 1974, during which Kingston Polytechnic's student group, Thames Productions, toured Cornwall with a production of *Charley's Aunt*. We camped on windy sites with few facilities sleeping ten to a tent (in tents borrowed from the local Scout troop). Despite these somewhat spartan conditions, the Hon Nick managed to smoothtalk local landladies of boarding houses into allowing him to take baths in their rather more salubrious establishments than the conditions those of us without a title and a golden tongue were forced to suffer!

After a fortnight in these circumstances, eating lumpy porridge and mackerel curry from enormous Scout cooking pots, we are amazed that young Nick can state he is inexperienced at al fresco eating and sleeping!

To the Queen, contributed by its author:

Dear Madam,

I know you are very busy but please can you tell me how I can get a dorgi? I think you invented them and I would like one too. Do you do it by marrying a corgi and a sausage dog? Please tell me.

Yours sincerely,
Rosemary Brown

And in reply:

Windsor Castle

Dear Miss Brown,

Thank you for your letter of 14 June. The only details I can give you about the crossing of dachsunds and corgis by the Queen is that Her Majesty uses a long-haired dachsund.

To Nigel Rees after a radio item on the art of playing tunes on one's teeth:

Edinburgh
7th February 1977

Dear Mr Reece,

Well, my illusions – if not yet actually my teeth – have finally been shattered! This morning about 8.40 whilst listening to the *Today* programme, the grim reality was borne home to me that what I had always hitherto considered my own unique gift, my own personal contribution to the development of Western Phonics, was not unique at all, but an accomplishment shared by others too: I am, of course, referring to your interview with one Mr Philip Shuttleworth on . . . playing one's teeth, a subject near to my heart, not to mention my palate. Before, though, continuing, one crucial point essential to professional esteem: one is not 'tapping one's teeth', one is playing – on an analogy with the xylophone – an *odontophone* (Gr. odous, odontos, a tooth; Gr. phone, a sound).

Anyhow, as one odontophonist to another, I was wondering if I could take the opportunity – I'm going to in any case! – to raise some points with you.

First of all, in all sincerity, I was most impressed by the virtuosity – accuracy and speed – with which you played the 'William Tell Overture' a piece I've been trying to master for quite a while. How much do you practise?

Being rather impatient by nature I tend to flit from tune to tune rather than perfect a few. So how big is your repertory? And to get the speed, when you say you use two fingers – as for Mr Shuttleworth's *thumbs*, well, how vulgar! – are they the index fingers of both hands, or the index and middle finger of one? I find the second preferable; also (my two front teeth are tuned one semi-tone apart which facilitates trills, if only I could build up speed).

I wonder also how many octaves you can reach; in my case it's two, and I've developed a fancy arpeggio to demonstrate.

Finally, a suggestion as to public performances. Clearly the odontophone is not very loud; also, getting the giggles halfway through the first movement of Beethoven's Fifth rather mars the majesty of the piece . . . and this (I find) tends to happen in front of an expectant audience.

So – the thing to do is to tape record the pieces beforehand and then, by turning up the volume quite a bit, a whole room can be filled easily with melody. Everyone can hear; the odontophonist's performance cannot be ruined by an infectious smirk; the cause of Art triumphs. I have no doubt that the Albert Hall could resound to the tap of teeth, and concertos written for odontophone and orchestra. Today, a few friends . . . tomorrow, the dentist's!

Best wishes,
Yours truly,
Michael Gold

Copies of this letter were sent to each member of the Oxford Boat Race crew when it was announced they were taking aboard a female cox, Sue Brown:

Dear 1981 Boat Race Oxford Crew Member

A BIOLOGICALLY SHAMEFUL OCCASION

Every stroke of your oar was a stroke to deny, defeat, shame and frustrate your brother man to whom you had denied the opportunity to be cox and honour his manhood on an occasion as great to him as to you, although you used it to disgrace, shame and deny him his due experience.

Occasion and the opportunity your creator gave you in making you men, was turned to dishonour and shame. The Eight won for Oxford at the price of the honour they owed to manhood. What silly oaf decided to dispense with your male cox?

Females do not understand knightly honour, and would volunteer to be Knights of the Round Table if they were permitted to, but the honour of manhood is as much in brotherhood and comradeship as in deed, and your acceptance of your cox's rejection will follow you through your life as disgraceful betrayal of comradeship and manly brotherhood. As much an insult and slap in the face as if King Arthur had rejected a qualified candidate for knighthood and appointed a woman instead. God who made you man to do your best for man, will judge the appalling disgrace you were party to inflicting upon your male cox – a disgraceful blot upon male honour and comradeship.

Woman's place of service is home and family welfare. To allow her to intrude upon the action and glory of manly exertion, at the expense of a fellow offends human honour and evolution much as if in the 1914 war a group of warriors had allowed a comrade tried in battle and desiring to continue in the role to be replaced by a silly Selection Board by his sister with her head full of fancies and neglecting the family to displace her brother and prevent the honour which was coming his way for playing the manly part. Qualified by nature and will to join in the fray but disqualified by caprice and fancy.

Before she knows, and takes her natural part woman will in ignorance and for fancy and amusement, try to take the male role, but here it is the duty of man to teach her and direct her to her own way and not encourage fancy in ignorance.

I trust I have made the complicated moral responsibility clear to you, and am sorry this letter had to be criticism instead of praise.

To comedienne Victoria Wood:

Southampton
17.1.82

Dear Victoria,

I was most concerned for the safety of the children on your programme tonight.

Please never carry anyone in a cardboard box or leave tots unattended on a settee.

To the Programme Director of BBC Television:

Christchurch, Dorset
27th March 1981

Sir or Madam,

I see you are promoting this Clare Francis again. And yet again!

I am a schoolteacher and a world traveller. One of my ancestors, in the Nineteenth Century, was the Captain of a Tall Ship. He must be laughing in his grave.

Sailing a boat – thanks to Man's inventive genius – has now become so simple that even a woman can do it. So why labour the point?

A woman friend of mine has just been visited by her son's girl friend. She is twenty three and BOASTS that she can't even boil an egg. Can she steer a boat? I forgot to ask.

What is the sense of encouraging girls to lead adventurous lives when there are not even enough career opportunities for boys? You are simply multiplying the number of disgruntled people – dooming them to future frustration.

I lived for twelve years in North America. Female emancipation there has led to the most appalling results and much unhappiness for both sexes.

I would like to see you giving girls encouragement in those fields that promote traditional values and thereby lead to community harmony.

To David Steel from a gentleman whose letterhead included the title 'Man of Vision':

London NW3

12th October 1981

Dear David Steel,

In all the years that I have been a Spiritual Healer, Nobody, I repeat Nobody has returned to me a Holy Gift which I had sent them. You David Steel have done just that. I am 78 years of age and I was shocked and deeply hurt. But as my love for Humanity is so great I forgive you. I shall as a Man of Honour, continue Interceding for your Long Life and Good Health, also for the success of the Liberal Party at the next General Election. I would add that I seek no favours nor have I any Ulterior Motives in sending Holy Gifts.

All of those to whom I have sent a Holy Gift have replied with thanks and kindness at my thoughtfulness. Below I give you some of the names, and if you want proof of what I say I'll be happy to show you.

His Holiness Pope John Paul II, King Juan Carlos, Prince Charles and Princess Di, Dom Mintoff, Duke of Buccleuch, Lord George Norrie, Anwar-El-Sadat, Margaret Thatcher, Lt. General J. Venezuela, Kjartan Gudmunnsoson and many more. David Steel, remember my words of wisdom. Be Kind, Be Understanding, Be Sympathetic, Be Forgiving, and Be a Good Listener.

God's Blessings be Upon you and all members of your Family. Now and always.

This poem graces the front of a postcard which shows a chocolate-box picture of a rural English scene, complete with village church. It was sent to poet Philip Larkin:

England Our England

Their – still local, still English! – church choir voices sang,
I think of saints and sinners.
But all I heard was England.
All I heard and saw were the green reeds by a river . .
and the river
and a meadow by the river . .
And I heard and saw and felt was England, England . .
– and the ceaseless night and day destruction of England

All I heard and saw and felt was our dear England, and our English people
– being 'eaten alive' . . .
The Church (for the sake of 'universal love' and the economy (of course) would ban all such anguish, all such agony, all such tears) – for England, and the English, for our country and our people. But it wasn't the small, ancient, candle-lit village church, of course, that suppressed my tears that night,
It was 'quiet', 'decent', 'respectable', '*English*' 'good' manners . . .

And on the other side:

Some advice to David and Elizabeth Emanuel, just before the wedding of HRH Prince Charles and the Lady Diana Spencer:

London
9th April 1981

Dear Mr and Mrs Emanuel,

I hope you will accept this letter in the spirit of helpful criticism in which it is offered – as an admirer of the Royal Family and the example they set us all in their lives (as I am sure you are too) and as an admirer of your clothes.

I know you have the exciting privilege of making Lady Diana Spencer's wedding dress, which naturally will remain a secret until the day. But I, and a great many people I hear discussing it (but perhaps not as bold to write as I am!), have been greatly worried by speculative sketches in the papers of completely off-the-shoulder styles, in the manner of the black dress you made her for the Opera evening.

Surely these styles do not reflect her real character of modest unspoilt youth and freshness which is her whole strength and charm? She has made such a hit with the public at large with her simplicity of dress that to clothe her (as at the Opera) as a sophisticated and much older 'woman of the world' spoils this image and is out of character (and of course black at Court is anyway traditionally sensibly reserved for the fairly frequent occasions of mourning).

So I, and a vast number of others, do so hope you will allow her to follow her own good sense and show a much needed example of decorum and real chic – especially at the most momentous day of her young life, when she will embody the hopes of a nation for a better and more stable world.

With all good wishes
from a Wellwisher.

To writer Hunter Davies after he'd written a piece in Punch *about the long, long running time (about four hours) of the film* Reds:

Dear Mr Davies,

You are quite right about *Reds*. My wife began to have contractions towards the middle of the film (she was already pregnant when we arrived). No problem, we thought – when the film ends in an hour or so we'll just go home, pack a suitcase and get off to hospital.

By the time Diane Keaton was trudging across the tundra, however, and Warren Beatty preaching revolution to the Muslims I was getting seriously alarmed. Visions of calling the cinema manager for plenty of hot water. Did the cinema *have* hot water? What was it for, anyway?

Luckily we got to the hospital in time – just. But I shall keep a close eye on the baby's political development.

*Could a humourist ask for a better letter of appreciation than
this – sent to Michael ffolkes:*

Dear ffolkes,

I have just seen your cartoon (page 982) in this week's Punch.
    Ha, Ha, Ha, Ha, Ha, Ha, Ha, Ha, Ha, Ha, Ha, Ha, Ha, Ha, Ha,
Ha, Ha, Ha, Ha, Ha, Ha, Ha, Ha, Ha, Ha, Ha, Ha, Ha, Ha, Ha,
Ha, Ha, Ha, Ha, Ha, Ha, Ha, Ha, Ha, Ha, Ha, Ha, Ha, Ha, Ha,
Ha, Ha, Ha, Ha, Ha, Ha, Ha, Ha, Ha, Ha, Ha, Ha, Ha, Ha, Ha,
Ha, Ha, Ha, Ha, Haaaaaaa, aaaaaaaa, Ho Ho Ho Ho Ho Ho Ho
Ho Ho Ho Ho Ho Ho Ho Ho Ho Ho Ho Ho Ho Ho Ho Ho Ho Ho Ho
Ho Ho Ho Ho Ho Ho,o,o,o,o, uuuuumm.........
                              Yours breathlessley,
                                 D. Woolland (Mr)
PS This letter could possibly be used as a reference.

If you ever come across a character in a Len Deighton novel putting away a lot of vintage champagne it just could have something to do with this:

Rheinberg
19th October 1976

Dear Mr Deighton,

With great interest I read your book *Yesterday's Spy*.

As I noticed you have mentioned the product UNDER-BERG within this book five times. I like to thank you very much for your indirect advertising my product.

In the meantime I ordered my subsidiary in London to send you some cases of it. So you have enough personal stock. In case you run out of it some time in the future please let me know.

With my best regards and many thanks for your interest in my product I remain

Sincerely yours,

(Deighton points out, by the way, that the references in his book to Underberg were almost entirely derogatory!)

This was sent to Richard Mabey, together with a photograph of a half-eaten book jacket:

Eton College
Windsor
29th September 1976

Dear Mr Mabey,

I was lucky enough to be given a copy of your delightful and fascinating book *Food for Free*. I am also lucky enough to have the use of a primitive cottage on the West coast of Scotland which, alas, I can only use for eight or nine weeks a year. So it sits empty for much of the year, empty, that is, except for the mice which come in for comfort and culture. Unfortunately, they misunderstood your title, and, as you can see from the enclosed photograph, had several free meals off your book. Fortunately, they left the text intact.

Do feel free to use the photograph for advertising purposes – provided I get 10% of subsequent royalties to enable me to control the mice immigrant problem.

As soon as your face pops up on television, your voice on radio or your name on a book jacket, so do all sorts of spectres from your past. Headteachers who loathed you at school invite you back to present the prizes. Former colleagues whose names you had just, thankfully, forgotten, phone up and ask you to get them a job. Complete strangers come up to you in pubs and tell you stories that begin: 'You probably won't remember me . . .'

Sometimes, though, the encounters are welcome – if, at first, a little embarrassing. Jack Trevor Story, for instance, had for years believed himself to be not just an orphan but completely bereft of living relations. In his, then, regular Guardian newspaper column he started to write about his dimly-remembered family. Free from having to consider the feelings of the people he portrayed, his imagination provided ever greater and more scurrilous embellishment. Until one day up popped a sternly censorious Aunt Ruth to put the record straight:

Dear Jack Story,

I received your article from a member of my family of which all the surviving members known to me are proud to bear the name 'Story' as inherited from Thomas Story, my father. Your satirical – in fact cynical – article, erroneously described Thomas Story as going bankrupt. Neither at the time did the family 'Live like Lords'. Thomas Story – himself a saintly man who spent his time and money throughout his life in devotion to God and service to man – retired to the country in 1907 owing to ill-health. He lived there simply and, with four children still of school age, he managed as a skilled craftsman to be almost self-supporting, but did receive a little help from the elder sons – and yes, we did have codlin apples!

Your father, Jim, we remembered as a lively lad, always ready to entertain younger members of the family with slapstick comedy or magic lanterns, full of fun and zest for living and without any of the psychological complication of youth today.

'Skivvy' is an inappropriate word to use of your mother at any time. She had a good family background – I use the word 'good' without snobbish implications. I remember her as a sweet and gentle girl who met my brother at Bible class.

There is never any justification for war, but your father died in World War I to give you the sort of freedom you now enjoy as you write for press and TV.

Surely this makes it an even greater onus on you to write only that which is true, either by implication or fact, seeing that of God in every man rather than destroying by cynicism. You say it was 'all hearsay, just a name', – perhaps these few facts may give your picture a new perspective.

Yours sincerely,
Ruth (née Story)

Sometimes these blasts from the past cast an ominous shadow over the victim's present. This was sent to Henry Root ... lucky, in this case, that his real name is William Donaldson:

Dear Mr Root,

I have recently read and enjoyed your excellent book but I am rather puzzled as to why the personal information about you on the dust-jacket is so vague. The reason that I write is that some 15 years ago I had occasion to spend a very enjoyable holiday in Dawlish. I was accompanied by my sister, the then Ellen Thompson, and her fiancé.

We arrived in Dawlish on the Saturday morning and were soon ensconced in our holiday chalets. Everything went smoothly until the following Tuesday evening. That was the night my sister, whilst admittedly under the influence of a not inconsiderable amount of alcohol, was lured (I do not use the word lightly) away from her chalet by the questionable charms of a young man, who, along with several other louts, was holidaying in an adjacent chalet.

To cut a long story short, the result of this illicit liaison is sitting approximately four feet away from me at this precise moment in time. Yes, you've guessed it, my fifteen-year-old nephew Brendan.

It was not until several weeks after the holiday that my unfortunate sister became aware of her unhappy condition. Of course by this time the young man had 'flown the coop', leaving no forwarding address.

Now at this very moment you are either breaking into a cold sweat or wondering why I'm writing. I'll explain: the only thing we ever knew about this blackguard was his surname, Root. (Although to be honest we thought it was spelled R-O-U-T-E) and, as I previously mentioned, we've just purchased your book. Two + Two = ?

Now I won't beat about the bush. I want some quick answers: (1) Have you ever been to Dawlish? (2) If so, was it in July 1965? If you've just answered yes to the above questions I won't be asking a third – at least, not in writing. My fists will be doing all the subsequent talking and if I tell you that I represented Wales in the 1972 A.B.A. Championships you could be forgiven for feeling more than a trifle apprehensive.

I await your confirmation/denial with interest. If I do not receive an acknowledgement within 21 days I will take your silence to be an acknowledgement of your responsibilities and you can look forward to me arriving on your doorstep soon after. I assure you that should the confrontation arise you will find it a severely distressing experience.

Yours grimly,

Writer Jeffrey Bernard may have wished he *had used a pen-name when he placed this letter (a satirical comment on the fashion at the time for writing biographies about the Blooms-bury group) in the* New Statesman *in 1975:*

July 1973

Sir,

Michael Joseph have asked me to write my autobiography and I'd be grateful if you could give me any information about my whereabouts and behaviour between 1960 and 1974.

Jeffrey Bernard

This is one of the replies – sent from Toronto:

Dear Jeffrey Bernard,

I can tell you what you were doing on the night of the Chelsea Arts Ball in 1963, Mr Bernard, because although some of the events of that night are a little blurred in memory I know that Winston and Jemima arrived just nine months later. They are beautiful children, Mr Bernard, though I think Winston must have your nose. You were wearing a false nose that night, you'll remember. All our family have classic profiles. The children often ask me about Daddy and now I'll be able to tell them we'll all be going to see you soon.

This, from former Daily Mirror *editor Mike Molloy, was another:*

Daily Mirror,
London
11th July 1975

Dear Mr Bernard,

I read with interest your letter asking for information as to your whereabouts and behaviour between the years 1960–74.

On a certain evening in September 1969 you rang my mother to inform her that you were going to murder her only son.

If you would like further information I can put you in touch with many people who have enjoyed similar bizarre experiences in your company.

Yours sincerely,
Michael J. Molloy

The mornings after Bernard's nights before often brought an ominous postman's knock. This is framed on his bedroom wall:

THE SPORTING LIFE
4th October 1971

Dear Mr Bernard,

It will come as no surprise to you that following your unpardonable exhibition at the point-to-point dinner which you attended as a representative of this paper on Friday evening, it is no longer possible for you to continue in our employ.

This was not, you will agree, the first time your behaviour has compromised us and to protect myself and all connected with *The Sporting Life* from further embarrassment I have no alternative but to terminate your engagement forthwith.

Although in the circumstances I do not consider there is any onus on us to pay you three months' salary in lieu of notice, I am giving you the benefit of any doubt that may exist and you will be hearing from our cashiers in due course.

I am sorry that this has become necessary but you will agree you were given every chance.

Should you wish to return to this office to collect any personal belongings, I would be glad if you would arrange with Mr Sandys to do so and I would be obliged if you would return to me your metal press badge at your earliest convenience.

Yours faithfully,
C. W. Fletcher
Editor

Mr Fletcher wrote me this letter in reply to my request to publish his first one:

Dear Ms. Carter,

Thank you for your letter of September 22.

The letter I sent to Jeffrey Bernard wouldn't mean a great deal without the background to it.

He had agreed to present *The Sporting Life* trophy to the leading woman rider at the annual point-to-point dinner. As reported to me, he fell out of his taxi on arrival, staggered around at the reception until passing out and was left sleeping on a settee when the company went into dinner.

My then-deputy, who was present in a private capacity, had to step into the breach, make a speech off the cuff and also try to explain away J.B.'s alcoholic inertia. He was not well pleased and later gave me a 'him or me' ultimatum. On that there was no betting . . .

If Jeffrey agrees to publication of the background, I will agree to publication of the letter!

Yours sincerely,
C. W. Fletcher

This one came from Alan Hall, former diarist at the Sunday Times:

Sunday Times
London WC1
1973

My Dear Jeffrey,

Your red jumper, which does not come from Fortnum and Mason, is safely locked away in one of my secret drawers.

Do not try to get hold of the mad vicar – he telephoned me on Saturday and I interviewed him nigh unto death.

Do not try to get hold of me because I very likely will go on the piss today and to the races tomorrow.

Do not try to get hold of yourself, we've all tried it and its impossible.

I shall never stop regarding you with astonishment and affection.

Yours ever,
Alan Hall

This student has some pretty elementary research to do before she gets the high result she seeks. It was sent to the writer William Trevor:

Dear Mr Trevor,

At school I am doing a Project of 9,000 words each on two famous authors, Ms J. B. Priestley and your goodself.

Sir, to assist me achieve the high result I seek with my work would you please oblige me with a short list of your likes and dislikes, personally signed. I am hoping to be able to contact Ms Priestley with the same request.

Andrea Newman, author of those steamy novels Bouquet of Barbed Wire *and* Alexa, *has also had her sex changed by a correspondent. Curiously (and Ms Newman says rather worryingly!) this letter came* after *the recipient had done a lengthy interview on the radio!*

Edgware
Middlesex

Dear Mr Newman,

I was listening to the broadcast you made on Sunday morning about truth being stranger than fiction. Well I have been a victim of this phenomena and I could tell you some astounding things what have happened to me, for no other reason than that my ex-husband's brother was a civil servant, who clan together to make life difficult for the person they wish to deprave. Never in my wildest dreams did I think this could ever happen to me but unfortunately it has. When I heard your broadcast I got in touch with the BBC and they very kindly gave me the number of your agents. However when I phoned your agents they told me you were an extremely busy man and would I write and they would send the letter on to you. So I am asking you please could you spare me about one hour of your precious time to prove this is valid. I now have a lead. If you cannot spare the time please could you put me in touch with a person who is as knowledgeable as yourself.

This writer, from Belfast, also thinks she's got wind of something fishy . . . The letter was sent to the editor of a woman's magazine for which (the very female) Claire Rayner is Agony Aunt:

Belfast
8.1.75

Dear Sir/Madam,

This may seem like a strange request, but would it be possible for you to tell me if Claire Rayner is just a pen-name, and could it be possible that Claire Rayner is a man?

A reply would be greatly appreciated as this question would settle an argument in our household, since my daughter claimed that she met a man at a dinner-dance here in Northern Ireland, who claimed to be this Particular Writer.

Your advice in this matter would be greatly appreciated.

Mrs Lynda Chalker, MP once received a letter from a member of her own department which addressed her as Lynda Chalker Esq. Her department, incidentally, is that of Health and Social Security. She also received one, from a constituent, which addressed her as H.R.H. Lynda Chalker.

More usually, constituents elevate themselves to royal status. Winston Churchill, MP recently got a letter from a gentleman claiming to be the rightful King of England. He seemed happy, however, to allow the present incumbents of Buckingham Palace to remain in situ – so long as he was provided with suitably regal council accommodation. This constituent, one of Michael Meacher's, is less accommodating:

Dear Sir,

I wish to draw your attention to a proven fact, rife in your constituency. The Oldham Hulme Grammar School has proved by search of existing records that there is a legal Queen of England namely Hilda Carr of the above address. This makes Elizabeth Mountbatten and her ancestors back to Prince William of Orange illegal.

These facts should be given to the press without delay. Will you kindly see that this is done. A police court case was held in Rochdale some time ago proving that Queen Hilda (myself) is the legal Queen of England. Rochdale and Littleborough police have proof and knowledge of these facts. Please deal with this matter promptly.

Queen Hilda I

This is a matter not of mistaken identity but of mistaken geography. This letter was sent to Poet Laureate Sir John Betjeman by his friend, Rupert Alec-Smith:

Dear John,

Thank you for your postcard of Penarth. Professor Garner Rees of Hull University who was made a D.Litt – as you are – of Hull at the same time as myself, knew a professor, D.Sc., who lived in South Wales and was blamed by his wife that he neglected their children and spent all his time in his laboratory at Cardiff University. So it was agreed between them that on Saturdays he would give his work a rest and take the children to Penarth. A friend calling at the lab one Saturday found the professor and his children with him. 'But I thought,' he began, 'you always took the children to Penarth on Saturdays.'

'Shut up, you fool,' the professor whispered, 'the children think this *is* Penarth.'

Hunter Davies made himself unpopular when he included the name of fellow writer Leslie Thomas in his Book of Lists. *The list in which Thomas appeared was 'Great Bastards'.*

After apologies had been demanded, and made, Thomas wrote this:

Dear Hunter,

Thank you for your note. I am glad to accept your apology and pleased that the matter is being cleared up. Since it is, I have to tell you that there were those quite near and dear to me who would agree with you. My agent, Desmond Elliott, went so far as to offer – if the matter came to court   to give evidence for the defence!

In fact, naming names is always a dangerous thing for writers to do. Colin Reid once wrote a Daily Mail *column entitled 'The Private Life of D. Know, Esq.' about the people who tick the 'Don't Know' box in opinion polls. It drew a picture of an inadequate and worried ditherer. Two days later the paper's Editor received this:*

Chester

Sir,

Regarding 'The Private Life of D. Know Esq.' (by Colin Reid) I *am* D. Know. I have a lined brow (furrowed as you put it). I part my hair down the middle, and have done for nearly 30 years.

It is all too easy for anyone acquainted with me to identify me from this article and as I am well known in Kent, in Derby and in Chester I take a serious view of this article.

If it were about one of the hundreds of Smiths or Joneses it would not be so serious, but I am the *only* D. Know in the country.

My wife and I are proud of our name. We can usually manage to cope with the small-minded people who make the time-worn remarks when being introduced.

I do not, however, expect to have to cope with an unusual increase of these, as I have had to cover the last 24 hours, and which I directly attribute to your article. (My job as a production superintendent is hard enough without having to cope with this.)

To say that I am disgusted and annoyed is an understatement and I will have to consider any future development that arises.

D. E. Know

The historical novelist Dorothy Dunnet discovered another pitfall for the unwary writer – unintentional obscenity. In one of her books, Queen's Play *she uses as chapter headings direct quotes from an old English translation of the Ancient Laws of Ireland. One of them includes the words: 'equestrians, and chariot-drivers, jugglers and buffoons, and podicicinists . . .' The last word does not appear in ordinary dictionaries, and prompted a letter from a London University Librarian, Alan Wesencraft, asking its meaning. He guessed it could be derived from the Latin words for 'buttocks' and castor oil. He was right. Several letters and much research later he wrote triumphantly to Mrs Dunnett, enclosing a copy of a later translation of the Laws which included a footnote to the original sentence which said: 'Podicicinists, ie who perform brugederacht out of their rears.' Mr Wesencraft wrote:*

The Gaelic word 'brugederacht' I cannot find in any Gaelic dictionary and I am rather guessing at the meaning, but I think my conjectural derivation (in my first letter to you) from the Latin is correct.

I am trying to think of a euphemistic circumlocution in case you are asked to explain again. On the other hand why not settle for the good old English expression 'break wind'?

Mrs Dunnett replied:

I have just cheered up my American publishers by telling them what they have printed on my behalf. Dwelly's Gaelic–English dictionary, by the way, gives all the variations of the word under 'bruchd'. The most famous exponent of the art, as you probably know, was Joseph Pujol, who performed at the Moulin Rouge at the turn of the century and could play the ocarina.

I have stopped using quotations in my chapter headings.

This letter was sent to actor Max Wall by his friend, playwright and scientist Eric Berger – an interesting up-date on the frontiers of technology:

Dear Max,

We have been pursuing some interesting new lines in the lab. Threswell arose on Xmas day convinced that a novel type of tea-strainer was possible employing Einstein's theory of curved space. We sedated the poor chap with a 20lb hammer and have heard little of his undoubtedly interesting views since. Work on an advanced solar collector employing microscopic threads of lasagne in a cheesy sauce, washed down with a litre of rough Chianti and followed by guavas and expresso coffee set us back £8.50 + VAT. We are considering moving the whole project to an Albanian take-away dirty raincoat franchise in Poplar.

Two from racing commentator Brough Scott's mail-bag:

Sir,

I thoroughly enjoyed your presentation of the York race meeting and was interested to learn that HADITOS was originally called HADITOFF but that the name was thought unseemly.

I wonder if Diamond Cutter would still be called such if it was realised that this is the term used by police in the novel *The Choir Boys*, to describe a particularly stiff erection?

Dear Sir,

I was interested to read in Brough Scott's racing column in your issue of 25th April that on the previous day the Guardian Classic Trial (1¼ miles) run at Sandown Park, had been won in a time of 'four minutes 4.78, just half a second slower than the new record . . .,

Was this the time taken by the winning horse to run 1¼ miles – or the jockey?

A celebrity – particularly one who appears on television – is public property. Like Stonehenge, only smaller. People who probably have perfectly good manners think nothing of walking up to someone they've seen on the box and peering into their faces from a distance of about four inches. Satisfied their identification is correct they call upon friends, spouses – anyone who's around – to take over the scrutiny. Very famous people tell me this ritual can even extend to physical probing – a squeeze here and there just to prove you really exist.

Less painful, but on similar lines, people write to the famous with incredibly bald requests. I'm sure Mrs Duncan of Chester wouldn't dream of walking up to a stranger and asking for some item of clothing. But she happily wrote to Frida (the raven-haired one in ABBA):

Dear Abba,

I won't beat about the bush – the jumper Frida wore when she sang Super Trouper – I would like it for myself as I admire it very much. I know a lot of others do too, but I thought I would ask for it. Here's hoping for a reply.

There's also a tendency to think the famous have infinitely large bank accounts (instead of practically infinite tax bills) coupled with some obscure obligation to help out the less fortunate. This letter was sent to writer Jeffrey Archer from an Irishman living in Scotland. Note the classic structure: the soften-up, the build-up, the crunch . . .

Dear Mr Archer,

Your television interviews and your amazing story have been a delight to me. As I write this letter I believe you to be a sensitive and very open-minded person. Without a doubt your endeavours are what adventure is made of and not taken to flattery you are what can be termed true genius, that indefinable quality that sets you apart from the average person. In many spheres of life your equivalent exists: Modigliani, Howard Hughes, Warren Beatty and even Julio Englesse, the Spanish singer number among those who I would class as genius to a certain degree.

Anyway you must be bored with character assessments like this and great story-teller though you are, can you now bear with me for a little story of my own. It's not an uncommon tale. I was born the product of a well-to-do working class family with all that implies. I did not particularly excel at school and left when I was sixteen to work for my father. It was not long till the feeling of total waste which now fills my life took root. By the time I was seventeen my father and I professionally parted.

Now aged twenty-six I am married and that feeling of waste has grown stronger. I find myself a prisoner of HP demands and nights out at the weekend. The only certainty is that my pools coupon has missed again and supposed happiness is the hard earned two weeks a year in sunny someplace. For the world's masses that is enough but for me I find the whole concept sadly lacking. Often I bury the urge to go hunting for El Dorado in the jungles of South America or go mining for opals in some remote country.

You must by now be wondering why you are reading this and where is the point. Well I am now going to ask you something quite outrageous. Would you consider giving me a lifetime interest free loan of £100,000? If so I would use the interest from the money to pursue what mattered to me. Before you die you will have likely accumulated enough money for a hundred lifetimes and if anybody deserves such wealth you as a total individual most certainly do. As I see it my only chance of escape to freedom is to have enough money or should I say power to do the things I have always wanted. If you consider my request ridiculous you would be totally justified then perhaps you may be able to give me a well paid job as your man in Brazil. None the less I remain a great fan.

The writer of this heart-tugging letter agreed to let me publish it if I would add the following PS:

If anybody else with fabulous wealth reads this letter and is sympathetic with my plight, please contact me through the author of this book.

(Please form an orderly queue – Ed.)

This was sent to Pat Phoenix, big-hearted Elsie Tanner in Coronation Street:

> Please take pity on us. My son is unemployed and has been for fifteen years. My husband's a cripple. I suffer from arthritis. We can't pay the food bills. The water comes through the roof each night . . . We both think you're so wonderful and we both watch you every night on our colour television.

And another:

> I think you're a lovely woman . . . you've a lovely face and a lovely figure. And I think you're a lovely actress.
>   Would you like to buy my bungalow from me for £20,000? I'll pay you back at £20 a week.

This was sent to Sue Brown, the first female cox to take part in the Oxford–Cambridge boat race:

> Newbury, Berks
>
> Dear Miss Brown,
>
> Congratulations to you on your being the first lady cox to the Oxford Boat Crew. May your part bring a successful win in the Race to come.
>   The reason that I am writing this letter is not only to offer my congratulations but also to offer yourself or the Oxford

University the chance to obtain an unique symbol of the Cox of the eight Man crew. The symbol is in the shape of an Austin 1100 K reg Motor Car to which is attached a number plate with the index number COX 80K, the plate is a very unusual one and during the past my wife and I have had several people, including individuals, who run exchange registration number firms, offer to purchase the car just for the prestige of owning the plate. Needless to say my wife and I have always turned down their offers simply because we had grown attached to 'our little car' as the wife would put it, but marriages get longer and families get bigger and so after many years of happy and troublefree motoring, we have finally decided to sell off 'our little car' and get ourselves a bigger 'our big car'.

You may think it a bit sentimental but my wife, myself and our children feel that 'our little car' should not go to just anybody or to someone who would just take the number plate and leave 'our little car' to die of rust in some scrapyard and when we heard the news that a lady cox had been chosen to cox the Oxford Boat Crew we thought who better to own the plate than yourself or Oxford University.

Please forgive me if it seems that this letter is a bit of a cheek but my wife and I felt that you or Oxford University may be interested. If so please write to us and let us know what you think.

PS 'Our Little Car' is old but runs well. I enclose a photo of its rear end taken in North Wales last year.

Same idea – rather more ambitious – To Jilly Cooper:

> Belmont Garage
> Edinburgh
>
> Dear Miss Cooper,
>
> We have just received a Gold Rolls Royce Silver Shadow which, because of its special registration number might be of particular interest to you.
>
> The registration number is 28 JMC and the mileage covered by the car is only just over thirty thousand.
>
> The care already lavished on this car is illustrated by the excellent condition and by the fact that the previous owner had the Spirit of Ecstasy gold-plated to match the rest of the car.
>
> The asking price for this vehicle is £18,750.
>
> Yours faithfully,
> T. Venelle
> Sales Department

To actress Carolyn Jones of Crossroads *from her bank manager:*

> Dear Miss Jones,
>
> I often think to myself that the history of your overdraft would make a suitable subject for a television series – what it might lack in dramatic interest would perhaps be compensated for by its potential for infinite continuity.
>
> Yours sincerely,
> J. Fiddy

Then there are people who feel that success is some tangible quality that may just rub off on them . . . if they can get close enough. These letters were sent to David and Elizabeth Emanuel, the designers chosen to create the Princess of Wales's wedding dress:

Chatham, Kent
4th October 1981

Dear Mr and Mrs Ammanual,

For a start forgive me if I have spelt your surname incorrectly as I see there are two ways in the dictionary.

With the trend of pantaloon trousers set by Her Royal Highness, The Princess of Wales, do you think it would be worth extending the fashion a bit farther if you got someone to make some long white socks and shoes with big brass buckles on them and you would nearly be back to how the men were dressed in Nelson's days.

I couldn't contact you direct because your phone is XD so I couldn't get the address of your home or premises. If you think the idea is worth a try perhaps you may give me a thought being an invalidity pensioner. I've also increased my knowledge by looking up your name and its meaning. That's another one for our rector's quiz in Church. I have to keep up to scratch with the Bible because of the awkward questions he flings out when he has these quizzes in Church.

Nigeria
February 1982

Dear Mr and Mrs Emanuel,

It is a pleasure to know about you and to correspond you and I hope this letter will meet you in fine physical and spiritual being.

I came across your address and your profession in a magazine and I so much admired the wedding gown you made for Diana Sphenster's wedding and I was writing to enquire of the possibilities of making one for me.

By God's grace I will be getting married this month my engagement is March and my wedding will be in May this year.

Please if you can make a similar complete wedding attire for me, ie everything that goes along with it, write me as soon as possible stating the price and the possibilities of me coming to London to collect it and/or supposing I send somebody for it?

My measurements are: BUST: 38", WAIST: 34", HIPS: 51".

God bless you. I look forward to hearing from you.

Dear David and Elizabeth,

Do you think my chances as a designer have any hope? I've doodled a few outfits, but I copied the heads and arms of each as I can't draw bodies but the designs are my own.

Just what career this (male) writer had in mind when he wrote to actress Mary Holland (Katie of the Oxo ads) it's difficult to say. Prize bull, perhaps?

Dear Mary Holland,

I hope you will not mind my writing to you but I like you very much.

How can I get into your Field? I have had experience in other Fields but never in yours. Please tell me the way in. I am very keen and some think I am good but I have not made a commercial yet.

The height of optimism is manifested by the proposers, one of whom wrote to Selina Scott of ITN:

I'd like to marry you, please, though I think to be fair to you it would be a good idea if we met first.

He went on to give date, time and place.

Pat Phoenix got this enticing offer, from a man who lives in Stark Adder Maines:

Will you marry me? I would like to sit with you in my cottage and you could cook me cowheel pie while I watch you on TV.

Even more hopeful than that — this, to Erika Rowe, the stunning nineteen-year-old girl who stopped a rugby match when she streaked across the pitch at Twickenham:

Erika,

You are wonderful! Join me on a 6 week Caribbean fun cruise – all expenses paid – starting on 23 January.

Please reply through the Personal Column of the Daily Telegraph as soon as possible, quoting TREBOR X20, so that we can meet and fix details.

Also to Erika Rowe, but with something rather different in mind:

Dear Erica,

For TRUE ADVENTURE and LASTING FUN – become a real, Bible-believing CHRISTIAN!

All the Best in 82,

This was to magician Paul Daniels:

Droysden
Manchester

Dear Sir,

I am 14 years old and I am a junior member of the Order of the Magi.

I was very interested in your request in Abracadabra for ideas for your forthcoming trip to Las Vegas.

Having given this matter much thought and due consideration I respectfully suggest that you take me along on this trip so that my brains will be 'on tap' for whenever you need them. I will make myself available at all times.

Requests to open fetes, make speeches and give charity concerts come to the famous with monotonous regularity. This, rather ambiguous, invitation was sent to Cyril Fletcher:

Dear Mr Fletcher,

We have just under 200 beds in our hospital of which about 90 are for geriatric patients and the rest are for our mentally handicapped adults. I'm sure that both sections of our hospital would look forward to, and enjoy tremendously, being entertained by you. Please let me know when you could come.

Pat Phoenix once received this, from a country vicar in Cornwall:

Dear Madam,

My organ has recently collapsed and I would like to ask your assistance in raising it. If you could see your way clear to be present at a fund-raising we are organising on February 2, I would be most grateful to have you. I cannot pay a fee, of course, but I can promise a warm welcome.

Some people have a funny sense of humour . . . This was sent to the two girls in Abba:

Liverpool

Dear Agnetha and Annifrid,

I was wondering if anything has gone wrong for you since you became Abba. Funny things like tripping over on stage or TV or yawning whilst being photographed or filmed. Have you ever been splashed by a car, run down or stopped by police for reckless driving? I would like to know of anything like that please.

Love
Angela Bailey

PS Could you please print a picture of you two girls throwing a custard pie in Bjorn and Benny's faces? Of course the other way round would be more interesting.

Others make very tall orders. This was sent to Claire Rayner:

London E14

Dear Claire Rayner,

My wish is for you to tell me a written policy for peaceful coexistence and cooperation without armed forces in the enclosed first class stamped addressed envelope.

Another one to Claire Rayner:

Manchester

Claire,

Could you explain briefly about the first world war, who caused the war and what year.

Thank you.

To Claire Rayner:

Dear Claire,

I have been married nearly twelve months and I have a little boy six months old. My husband and I are constantly rowing and on a number of occasions he has beat and kicked me quite seriously. I am still desperately in love with him but feel I cannot go on living under this threat of violence. I don't know where to turn for help. Should I go back to him or should I live a life of misery without him. Please help me.

Yours desperately,

PS Please don't tell me to visit a marriage guidance counsellor as this is my husband's job.

To actor Peter Bull:

Pewsey, Wiltshire
29th August 1964

Dear Mr Bull,

When you come home, I want you to do me a favour. If you know any of your Lady Friends who are Artists and wear Ostrich feathers in their make-up costumes – if they have one or two soiled or broken ones I could do with them. You see, Sir, I have made a Pearly King and Queen costume, for Pewsey Carnival which is on September 19th and its one of the best in the West of England. All I am short of, is some feathers for the Queen's hat. Our Rector brought me one but one is not enough.

I saw Miss Hayley Mills had some lovely ones when she appeared in a Star Performance and also the Tiller Girl dancers wear lots of them. Do you know any of them?

I won't bore you any more, Sir, because I know you are a very busy gentleman.

To Police 5 *presenter Shaw Taylor:*

London N15

Shaw Taylor,

I require your assistance in locating my shopping trolley which I dropped at the 236 bus stop located at Mildmay Grove London N1 on the side of the street for the 236 bus destination Finsbury Park while being chased by a man with a knife. Date approximately 11th instant, May 1980.

The push trolley contained my (personal) tunes for my urgent use and entertainment during my melancholy moments – I do not wish to hear any more extracts of tunes on all the different radio stations. I wish to locate my push trolley soon.

To Francis Wilson, television weatherman:

London NW1

Dear Francis,

We used to think you were the best thing that ever happened to television but now you have got so confident in your job you don't make any mistakes, therefore, you are not so much fun to watch any more.

Could you please make one boob for us tonight, Tuesday August 15. If not, Thursday evening, as Sharon will not be able to watch it on Wednesday.

Yours in anticipation,
Barbara and Sharon

To Miss Christina Foyle of Foyle's book shop:

Burton-on-Trent
19th July 1980

Dear Sirs,

Please advise me if you can supply any of the under-mentioned books:

Author	Name of Book
Marquis de Sade	Violation of Justine
Signorelli, The Painter	Book of pictures of female figures – emphasizing the bottom
William Etty, Painter 1787/1849	Book of pictures of female figures – emphasizing the bottom.

Two more to Christina Foyle:

Dear Sirs,

A friend of mine asked me to send you a draft for £200 – to cover the cost of books, regretfully 'borrowed' about 1958–60. Inflation has been taken into account and a contribution has been added. For obvious reasons the person in question does not wish to be named. Would you therefore kindly acknowledge a confirmation of receipt of cheque to the address on the enclosed sae.

Dear Miss Foyle,

I should like to arrange some affaires which I personally did wrong in my life. About six years ago I have been working in your shop and I took some books without paying for them. About three years ago Jesus came into my life and now I want to put these affaires straight too. First I ask you for forgiveness and want to pay the expenses of the books very generously.

Hoping that you accept my forgiveness.

To Jilly Cooper:

Clifton, Bristol

Dear Jilly,

Four years ago, as a partial wedding present I gave my wife *How to stay married* by a certain Mrs Cooper.

We haven't succeeded.

This evening as we went through our bookshelf making two neat piles, the only controversial book that doesn't seem to want to be divided is yours. What do you suggest we do: cut it in half?

Look forward to your advice.

An unusual request for Rolf Harris:

Newport Pagnell
Bucks.
6th February 1982

Dear Mr Harris,

Can you tell me, does a female kangaroo have a pouch when it is born? I have looked in my encyclopaedia but I could not find out.

Yours truly,
Simon Tang

Comedian Benny Hill was puzzled by a batch of letters he received from Greek fans when his show was first televised in that country. What puzzled him was that – although they came from different people, in different towns – every one said exactly the same thing. Right down to the spelling mistake:

Dear Benny,

I'm one of your greatest fans and I'm living in Greece and I know that it would be rather difficult for you to send autographs abroad but my hottest dream is to have an autograph of you dedicated to me. Well, I give you all my admiration and I am waiting, impratiently, for my dream to come true.

Hill finally discovered the explanation. He was in receipt of the first-ever all-purpose, pro-forma fan letter. It was printed, in English, in a Greek fan magazine. All the sender had to do was address it to the celebrity of their choice!

Most letters from overseas admirers, however, are distinctly original. This one was sent to actor Robin Bailey:

Argentina
August 1972

Dear Robin,

I have the pleasure to address to the magnificent great Actor that you're for greet and congratulate you for your excellent actuation in the film *Blind Terror* directed by Richard Flieshcher.

There you delight with your exceptional Art again and you point out your Talent, pleasanting to the public that love and applaud, so for all those things I consider you my prefer Actor.

I'm your admirer and want you send me a photograph and with your autograph.

I wish you to have the letter and greatest regards from you. Waiting to be pleased. I want you many exites in your Bright Artistic career because its serving you right.

I say good bye to you dearly
and sincerely,
an admired.

A warm and personal approach to Esther Rantzen from George, in Libya:

Libya
22.17.80

Hello Esther,

Here comes the voice of someone you haven't meet him before in your life. But before I have something to say throw my love I have on you. I will first ask of your health and your condition living this time in Britain. I hope you are in good health as I am over here.

Now I want to tell you my feelings I have on you. First I became glad when I saw your picture and you are call Esther too. At first I was keeping a friendship with a girl call Esther. And now I will to become friendship with you, if you are not having boyfriend. I am a Ghanian working in Libya.

And I have made up my mind to come and stay in Britain. Because I want to enjoy life somewhere. Were I am living now there is no life. You can never get speak to a girl or women, even you can't get drink to drink or to enjoy yurself. Your picture I saw in the newspaper is with me. I hope you will give me your love and your heart and I will give you my. You can send me your picture with your lovely reply to me. I hope my love will meet your love. If you have boyfriend then you find me girl who is having a good character like yourself. I will like to end here. My needs will make you to think of me day and night. If you give me a good reply then our love will become greater. Because girls call Esther are good girls with luck. May God help you.

Your loved one
George.

To Peter O'Toole, from Japan:

> Dear Peter O'Toole,
>
> I red in the newspayper were you in Japan? Our family saw the film *Lawrence of Arabia* and your face gave me a mysterious feeling. May you keep going forward at a stately pace as befits a great actress.
>
> Japanese admirer

To Erika Rowe:

> Dear Erika,
>
> I would like to write to you as a pen pal, if you have know objections. We both could compare notes about our likes and dislikes and other aspects of life. I am very interested in politics of various nations, also all aspects of show business, cinema, recording industry. Erika will you please give me your opinion on these subjects. I will close for now until the next time.

This, from an admirer in Ghana, gave Anne Nightingale many uneasy nights. She was worried she might be left, literally, holding the baby:

Ghana

Dear Anne (Nightingale)

I got to know you from your London calling from a friend of mine. I was very grateful to see such a beautiful girl like you. As beautiful as I wish my future wife to be. I am also pleased to see such a young girl like your tipe in such a position, in the BBC world service.

I therefore like to chose you as my friend in London and like to be my sister as well. This may be wonderful to you for this may be your first time to have such a letter. But get take it that you are trying to help you poor brother who is suffering in Ghana. I have had my first born baby girl whom I have planned to name her after you. And if it is your wish let me know it early. As a poor messenger I am not going to marry the Mother that is why talked of future wife. For I cannot care for her and the child as I am receiving four cedis a day and spend about ten cedis a day. So you see we are facing hardships in Ghana.

I only like to name my child after you to help me develop the child in a way you think fit. Also I would like you to take the child away if it is your wish. Hoping to hear from you soon.

Your one,

De Graft, K.A. Trimpong

To Rachel Heyhoe-Flint from an Indian journalist she had met briefly at a formal dinner:

Dear Rachel Heyhoe (mrs Flint)

Let me record maximum appreciation for having correctly and cleverly identified me as the India Pressman spoken of by Miss M. Pascoe. Indeed I deem myself most lucky to have attended Friday's ever unforgettable lunch-function and made maiden contact with you at the heightened hour of your blaze and brilliance.

It would be more convenient if I talk to you here in London during your next early visit. I am wanting to leave towards the end of the month. We can meet in the *Daily Telegraph* building or I can invite you at the nearby place of my frequent stoppings where we can chat with coffee and snacks. If Mr Flint (so sorry not sure of the first name) too joins, so far so better. Please therefore indicate by return mail whether you could make it by this weekend or at least before the Christmas. Telephone intimation can be given between 8.30–9 any morning but not afterwards as I am then always out until late midnight. In the meanwhile I shall be anxiously awaiting three–four wedding pictures (in different poses).

Here is one urgent and important query to answer in your reply. List of the Cricket Writers' Club shows not a single female name. I am surprised not to find even an established writer like your reputed self therein. Does the membership rules bar women? Women's cricket and its administration may be on separate footing, but female cricket writers must share the roof in Press Boxes and other bodies. This is my personal view. Kindly enlighten.

Please convey to Miss Pascoe how I met you on the big occasion and about this communication.

To athlete David Moorcroft, from West Germany:

Dear Sir,

May I extend today my very sincere compliments and congratulations on you and your own fine and outstanding track and field life and career in England.

I have been following always all my life so far Track nations and worldwide and thus became too very much delighted and thrilled and impressed with your life and career and successes and now your fabulous phantastic worlds record, 5000m in 13.00.42, that's sure phantastic, you will be then in future too the first man to run 5000m below 13 minutes, I am confident for you. Britain can really be always so really proud of you.

Today I'd like to ask you too a personal request and am really hoping that you will be so kindly to oblige. Please have the great kindness and do send me as lasting remembrance, one photograph of you, with your personally signed autograph and dedication on the photo please, truly signed by you too. Please have comprehension for my sportly plea.

Very cordially greetings and compliments, stay well and sound and happy and successfully there too in future with Mrs Linda and son Paul, looking really forwards too to hear very soon from you again from England.

> very sincerely and
> very sportingly yours,
> Gerd Riethenauer.

This was sent to the publishers of author Raymond Briggs:

Dear Sirs,

I am a fifth-year girl student of primary school. Lately I read a book what is called 'St Nicholas exceedingly sensitive to the cold'. As I felt very merrily, I wrote Mr Briggs a letter. Excuse me, but send this letter to Mr Briggs.

Your truly

And this was the letter that came with it:

Dear Raymond Briggs,

How do you do, Mr Briggs? I'm a Japanese girl twelve years old, I love *Father Christmas* and *Father Christmas goes on holiday* you wrote. I enjoyed lovely illustrations in them. Now I have become a junior high school pupil. I decided to write to you. By the way I have so many questions of you that I can't decided which to start. I afraid my questions confuse you. Let me see . . . what on earth are you? In short, are you tall? Are you fat? What color your hair? and your eyes? How old are you? (I'm afraid) In my image of you are a little fat old man with gray hair, and your bushy-bearded face is always smiling . . . just like Santa Claus in your books.

I have much to talk to you, my letter is becoming longer, I must stop now. I thank you for reading such a poor letter. And if you have time, would you write this little girl who loves you and your books so much? I don't care if this is one way. If you read this I am happy enough.

To William Donaldson:

Comrade Willie!

I am student of agricultural biology at university of Omsk, but work now in London as adviser to Russian trade delegation for pigs. I ask you help me.

I write thesis on fertilisation of carrot *(genus clupea ruberae)*. With new idea production of carrot can to increase three time in one year. Pig eating carrots give 23% more production of meat, and look better too. Every Sunday I make visitation to grave of our great leader Karl Marx. I believe he want me to share my discovery of carrot with all working people, not only working people of my country. Therefore I want to publish thesis in England.

They say you write in theoretical journal Planthouse. I do not know this journal but they say many people read. You work in Planthouse. You think Planthouse is interesting for fertilisation?

You like vodka, caviar? I am very boring in London. I know only pigs. We can to meet? We eat we drunk I say you about my work. I already receive workers 'Plashaya Riba' prize for my paper on cabbage production in Ukraine. Maybe this also good for Planthouse?

I like to hear you.

Your comrade in soil,
Koren Kubichevsky.